E

MW01089265

I have known Keith Ferrante and his wife Heather for more than 18 years. I love Keith's passion for equipping a generation of spiritual fathers and mothers and his vision for leaving a legacy for the next generation. Keith's new book, *Unlocking An Abundant Mindset*, is an inspiring story of his own journey into abundant life. With biblical teaching and real-life examples, he shares keys that will guide you into living out the Kingdom in every area of your life, especially in your finances. I highly recommend this book for anyone who wants to be free from a poverty mindset and become a Kingdom resource!

—Kris Vallotton
Leader, Bethel Church, Redding, CA
Co-Founder of Bethel School of Supernatural Ministry
Author of ten books including, *The Supernatural Ways of Royalty* and *Spirit Wars*

In Keith's latest book, *Unlocking An Abundant Mindset*, Keith invites us into his personal journey to observe how God shattered poverty mindsets which were restricting abundant life for Keith and his family. I am a personal witness to these real-life events. I have watched Keith become a successful, independent resource without breaking connection with the local church. Though this book has great keys for any person seeking the abundant life, I would consider it "required reading" for any of those called to itinerant ministry.

—Dan McCollam
The Mission, Vacaville, CA

International director of Sounds of the Nations, Mission School of Prophecy, co-founder Bethel School of the Prophets, and author of *Prophetic Company*

In *Unlocking An Abundant Mindset*, Keith Ferrante powerfully combines biblical truths with his personal experience to help obliterate restrictive poverty mindsets that hinder the fullness of God manifesting in us and through us. I highly recommend it.

—Steve Backlund
Bethel Church, Redding, CA
Founder of Igniting Hope Ministries

My friend, Keith Ferrante, has lived what he has written here in *Unlocking An Abundant Mindset*. As I read his book, I was reminded of struggling with similar circumstances, but Keith helped me think deeper about the solutions. The whole journey carries the reader to embrace an abundant, loving Father-God. I also found key statements that, by themselves, are worth the price of the book. For example, two statements that hit me especially hard were these: "Poverty is rooted in a lack of value and value is rooted in a depth of identity." "You can't achieve destiny in poverty . . ."

This book is a feast of faith, lifting the reader to the kingly mindset necessary for success.

—Harold Eberle
Yakima, Washington
Founder of Worldcast Ministries

Our life journeys are not always neat and easy; most often they are raw and messy and give us many opportunities for personal growth. Though each of us involved in the journey has their perspective on the facts, what is common is the commitment to live and love together through it all and let God challenge and transform our unhealthy mindsets. In his book, *Unlocking An Abundant Mindset*, my friend and fellow traveler, Keith Ferrante, uses his journey to share some powerful revelations that will help the reader identify and confront thinking that keeps them from living in abundance.

—David Crone
Sr. Leader of The Mission
Author of *Decisions That Define Us, Prisoner of Hope*, and *Captivated By the Expectation of Good*

UNLOCKING
an
Abundant
MINDSET

UNLOCKING
an
Abundant
MINDSET

• Keith B. Ferrante •

Published by: Keith B. Ferrante, 6391 Leisure Town Rd.,Vacaville, CA 95687

Cover Designer: Shelby Gibbs, www.shelbycreative.com
shel.bgibbs@gmail.com

Editing and interior layout: Creatively Inspired, LLC
www.creativelyinspiredlife.com

Printed in the United States of America

ISBN-13: 978-1544633350
ISBN-10: 1544633351

TABLE OF CONTENTS

ACKNOWLEDGMENTS

J'd like to acknowledge those who assisted in the initial formation of this book right on through to its publication:

- *Angie and Tom Parsons:* Thank you for the many long hours of initial preparation and first edits of this book. I'm especially grateful for your investment of prayer, exposing the enemy's tactics and releasing Heaven on my behalf that kept me walking victoriously so many times. What a huge blessing you have been to me personally, and I pray rich blessings on you both for your many sacrifices!

- *Jane Ferrante:* Thank you, Mom, for your fine-tuning contributions to this book. I thank God for you!

- *Carol Cantrell:* Thank you for being so thorough and bringing this book to its final completion. I so appreciate all your efforts!

I'd like to express my gratitude to those who helped me learn to become a resource:

- *David Crone:* Thank you for speaking into me as well as making room for me to grow and develop into the person I am. I will be forever grateful for you.

- *Dan McCollam:* Thank you for opening up many doors for me to speak, producing my first CDs, believing in me as a prophet, helping me get launched in my ministry, making the way for Emerging Prophets, and helping me to think like a resource. Your friendship has been invaluable.

- *Kris Vallotton:* Thank you for believing in me and opening the many doors that sent me to minister beyond my own range of influence. I'm so grateful that you believed in me.

- *Heather:* My lovely and faithful wife, thank you for believing in me. Without you, I would not be the resource I am becoming. You have stood by my side, fought for me, and helped in so many ways to advance all that I do. Your tireless efforts behind the scenes—doing so many significant tasks that build what we do and who we are—do not go unnoticed. I love you and am forever yours.

Thank you! I'm so grateful to God for you all!

DEDICATION

This book is dedicated to all those who, like me, began in a place of impoverishment, but lifted their vision heavenward believing there was something greater. May you find your way out of poverty, lack, and the drudgery of hard labor and discover the storehouse of wealth waiting for you that is also meant to bless others through you. May you find your promised-land inheritance and enjoy rest from all toil!

INTRODUCTION

*U*nlocking *An Abundant Mindset* targets several categories of people. It is primarily directed toward those individuals anxious to break out of their poverty mindset and step into becoming a resource for others. In addition, this book is designed to help emerging business leaders and established business leaders looking to discover and/or increase products and resources that utilize Kingdom multiplicity and abundance. Because I have spent many years as a pastor and an itinerant minister, I share experiences from my own unique journey about the mindsets of people in the vocational church world leadership and how I learned to think outside of a salaried position. I do believe this book will also be useful to every follower of the King, no matter the job or type of work you do, as you discover the keys to an **abundant Kingdom mindset** that is not restricted by limited resources.

How did all of this come about, you might ask? Well, let me tell you my story. It all unfolded one summer in a faraway island nation.

Slow-Paced and Laid Back

The Fijian islands are a place of captivating beauty. The 110 inhabited islands and over 500 islets that make up this nation consist of crystal-clear blue water, pristine beaches, and lush green landscapes. The people are joyful and hospitable; they love to share stories and just do life together. The pace in Fiji is leisurely, to say the least. In fact, the locals call it, "Fiji time".

Back in 2009, the leadership at The Mission Church in Vacaville, California, had been establishing strategic relationships and forging a wonderfully increasing Kingdom presence in Fiji for over a decade. I, too, had a strong desire to fortify and establish a culture of expanding revival in that nation. The locals in Fiji invited us from The Mission to partner in starting a 10-week supernatural school there, which would be the first of its kind on the islands. I was asked to lead the school, and I felt a tremendous sense of honor in accepting this position as well as a healthy weight of responsibility.

The school was a great success! For the first time, signs and wonders flowed through the hands of many Fijian people, prophetic utterances poured from their mouths, and many lives were powerfully transformed! We had discovered a new model of empowering lives within the structure of a short-term supernatural school. Up to that point, the established structure had been a one- to two-year ministry school, which was obviously much longer than a ten-week school. We experienced accelerated transformation in a shorter period of time. What a wonderful and impacting prototype we had discovered!

New Culture Experiences

Fiji had so many new experiences and exciting adventures

awaiting us. Wearing the national Fijian clothing, called the *sulu*, a kind of male skirt that most of the tribesmen wear, was a bit awkward and embarrassing at first, but the people loved that I wore it. For their hot and humid climate, the *sulu* is cooler and very comfortable.

As is true in most new places you visit, we found the native food a big stretch for us. We tried many traditional dishes, including turtle, which was first beaten to smithereens and chopped up right in front of our eyes. We had certainly never experienced anything quite like that before, and to our Western tastes, it was very unappealing. But actually, it wasn't too bad, even with its stringy texture. At first, the kids weren't too fond of the different food, and Fijian sanitary standards were also much less than what we were all used to; nevertheless, they seemed to adapt really well overall.

What I missed the most was Mexican food! It's always my comfort food. So whenever I leave home to travel to another nation, I always miss it. No Mexican food on the Fijian islands, that's for sure!

The Fijian people with whom we worked were very friendly, and their happy dispositions and smiles were so contagious and inviting. We spent that memorable summer enjoying the Fijian culture with all its unique distinctions and the many new adventures.

Taking a Financial Hit

Though our time there was marked with good times, it was also one of the most difficult financially. We had not anticipated our summer of teaching and ministering in Fiji would be so costly. Only a year prior, my family and I had left our hometown of Willits, California, where I had lived for 20 years, and moved to Vacaville, California to become a part of The Mission church and international ministry team—a dream come true for us. Never in my life did I think I would be doing anything but *pastoring* a local church. It had taken some processing with mentors to help give me permission to explore the dreams of my heart outside of functioning as a senior pastor. But the desire of my heart to travel to the nations and help raise up supernatural schools came to life once we moved there.

Fulfilling our dream was wonderful, but in the process of relocating to our new life in Vacaville, we had the burdensome task of selling our house. Unfortunately it didn't sell, and over a long period of time when the sales market was at an all-time low, we ended up foreclosing. That was a painful and costly sacrifice with which to enter a new day. It was especially painful because our credit plummeted after having such great credit for years. Although our ministry move really cost us, we were confident the Lord would one day bless us for that sacrifice.

During our first year in Vacaville, we lived in a rental house. Two weeks before going to Fiji, the owner decided he wanted his house back. Because of the short notice, and concerned we would not be able to get another rental house because of our poor credit, we put our household belongings into storage. Agonizing about this decision but trusting God, we proceeded to Fiji on schedule.

Upon our arrival, we quickly discovered our financial situation was about to take another nosedive, and what little we had would be stretched to the limit. It had been prearranged that the students' tuition payments would actually fund our living expenses there in Fiji. This was the only way we could have gone there to do our work with a family of 4. We soon learned, however, that virtually none of the students had the required funds to cover for their school fees. Only one person had the full tuition, and the rest had only about $10 each. This was not enough to take care of our family's living expenses *and* run the school. We spent the entire summer finagling finances, a bit at a time, just to make ends meet. With some of the students, we only got about half of the fees for the entire school course, and by the end of the summer, others had hardly paid anything at all. I had my share of conversations with the students to try and recoup the necessary fees to cover the expenses, but most never came in. It was clear that the students did not consider the prearranged financial obligation for their tuition a priority.

It was bittersweet, to say the least.

In order for us to make it through the summer, I had to spend all of my reserve money—the funds I had set aside to secure a rental home upon our return to the U.S. This lack presented a problem. I now had no rent money, and yet, we would need a place to live when we returned home. Intense anxiety was beginning to take ahold of me.

Revelation of a Poverty Spirit

I had several conversations with the Lord towards the end of that Fijian mission trip. I told Him, "Lord, I really, really love this school of the supernatural. I love the students . . . I love this nation . . . I just love doing this! But, please! I *never* want to develop a school this way ever again!" It was so exhausting trying to build a school, work with the students with each of their unique needs, teach every day, navigate through cultural differences, care for my family on foreign soil, *and* struggle financially to stay afloat the way we did that summer. I determined that any future opportunity would have to be much different.

Prior to going to Fiji, I was not familiar with their culture or their view of finances. I wasn't aware of how lax they were in follow-through with such a laid-back way of doing life. While I enjoyed interacting with the people and loved the privilege of engaging with the nation of Fiji, this growing experience was very painful for me personally.

In response to my complaints, the Lord said, "Keith, the reason the school is so frustrating is because the same spirit you are dealing with in them is also in you. If you don't want to do the school that way again, then I am going to have to remove the **poverty spirit** out of *you*." Ouch!

I began to examine the root foundation of the poverty spirit in my life. You see, I grew up in the church; my father was a pastor. I had lived within a model of poverty in the church, the same as many of my ministry friends with whom I had been connected. It was a mindset that believed and functioned in this way: *Being poor is spiritual. Those who serve God will have very little.* With this same mindset, I observed many pastors, leaders, and Christians in the church give so much of themselves in God's service with great sacrifice, exhausting their own personal financial resources to a painful degree. Many of them come to the end of their life with very little to show for it and with so much anxiety and concern about how they were going to live out their days. Living in such a way took a real toll on them.

With this revelation from the Lord, I knew that I had to change my own poverty mindset, but I honestly did not have a clue how to do that or what it would look like. Over the coming years, as God walked me out of that place, I discovered keys into Heaven's rich abundance. For this reason I wrote *Unlocking An Abundant Mindset* in hopes that as I share my journey out of a poverty mindset, you might also benefit.

How to Use this Book

I have included a section at the end of each chapter called "Questions to Ponder", giving you an opportunity to take some time to reflect on your own life. My hope is that it will allow you to go deeper as you consider your own present mindset, beliefs incongruent with New Covenant ways, and other areas that may be hindering the progression the Holy Spirit envisions for you. Allow for an unhurried time with the Lord that will provide for a genuine transforming encounter with Him. As you go through this book, have an expectation to move out of the place you're in presently and into a whole new level.

Let the Process Begin

So, here I was in Fiji, and now the Lord was confronting the poverty mindset deeply rooted within me, mirrored in the nation where I was serving. One of the major lessons I have learned over the years is that when I come into a nation where I've never been or travel to a different region or new city, God shows me something in myself that needs adjusting. Before I can influence that nation or city, the strongholds that have been a part of that region's behaviors and attitudes will find the places in me that are similar and need addressing. God is always after our greater development and transformation, and I have appreciated this as His wonderful gift in taking me higher and causing me to mature in areas that were stagnant or useless to Kingdom advancement. Sometimes that growth can be a difficult journey and can even come close to knocking a person right out of ministry. But I have come to appreciate the processes He walks me through in order to gain full freedom in the specific strongholds on nations or regions also affecting me.

Many of the Fijian people I was leading and sharing life with had unknowingly been living under a poverty spirit. But you can't achieve destiny in poverty. That summer of ministry began my own personal journey where the Lord took me out of agreement with that negative way of thinking and into a brand new season.

Offense kicked off that new season for me. It opened my eyes to understanding the poverty thinking I had lived with, and that is where my story begins.

One

FROM POVERTY TO POWERFUL

*M*y breakthrough out of poverty began as the result of an offense. While I was dealing with the financial issues in Fiji, I also became aware that I might not have a job when I returned back to the U.S. My job at our home church was to oversee the second year school of ministry. The enrollment was at an all time low as there weren't that many first year students who would continue on. When I became aware that our financial situation would possibly change due to the lack of students, I was offended.

My anxious thoughts ran wild: *Lord, don't you see all that I'm doing for You over here in Fiji? What is going on at home? What's happening to my income? I've spent so many years in the ministry for You sacrificially. And now here I am in Fiji spending thousands of dollars from my own personal funds, and this is my reward? . . . No job to go home to?* I was really offended by it all, distressed, and hurt.

Self-pity started to creep in and I felt myself beginning to spiral downward. I began blaming myself, blaming the leaders in Fiji, upset at the lack of students back home, blaming the whole church system—you name it, I blamed it.

A God-Setup

But what a great setup from God!

"How could this be a setup from God?" you may be asking. Well, this offense demonstrated that there was something inside of me that needed to be dealt with. What was it? I needed to be free from expecting people to be the primary source of my provision!

Offense can only hit us in a place we have not fully yielded to the Lord. God wanted me to look to Him as my source, not man. He was to be my sole provider.

You might also ask, "But wasn't there a valid reason to be offended in those situations?" Yes, of course! We will always find a "good" reason for offense. When we are offended, we feel like someone owes us—God owes us, people owe us, our leaders owe us, and so on. But the truth is, God is trying to expose an incorrect core foundation in our life, one which expects other people to *provide* for us instead of learning how to become a *resource* person who functions with a heavenly mindset of abundance and wealth.

This was a testing time for me personally. At this point I had to ask myself some honest questions: *Am I at my home church*

(The Mission) for the students, the staff, and the leaders? Or am I here because God has really called me? If I was here because God and I had dreamed about this, then God was the one I had to fall back on, not The Mission, the leaders, the school, the students, or anyone else.

You see, I have observed something for years. God brings people to an apostolic center like The Mission, and people will either become a resource for the Kingdom of God or get offended and be knocked out of commission by the challenges of breaking through a poverty mindset that says: *Those people are supposed to provide for me. When is someone going to recognize my gifts and acknowledge me? Why doesn't that leader see what I carry?* Such thoughts are endless and are a deeply rooted belief system.

The Power of Overcoming

Sometimes becoming a powerful person comes through overcoming offense. There is usually a lifestyle of offense connected to living in lack. Before we can rise up out of our present circumstances of difficulties and pressures though, we must determine that we are forever **done** with the way things are: *We are done with poverty. We are done with being a victim. We are done with being offended at what others possess that we don't.* We must get good and fed up with our present impoverished thinking if we are going to make a change.

Proverbs warns us of the dangers of offense.

> *A brother offended is harder to win over than a fortified city, and contentions [separating families] are like the bars of a castle.*
>
> 18:19, AMP

25

Offense has the potential to destroy us and become a barricade to our blessing. It can literally wall us in and shut us off from the flow of Heaven's abundance. But if we recognize that the offenses we encounter in life can actually become opportunities for rewards, we can turn those offenses around for our own good. In sports terms, we must learn to be on the offensive—be aggressive—in dealing with the spirit of offense.

Putting Someone on A Pedestal

Working through an offense can also help reveal people we may have placed on a pedestal, whether consciously or not. Once revealed, we may see that we have allowed individuals to hold the keys to our destiny instead of God. Yet He alone is the one who promotes, blesses, and opens doors for us. When we get offended because someone didn't respond the way we needed him or her to respond, that offense is merely showing us that we have given that person a greater position in our heart than God. Wherever we have allowed a person's influence in our lives above God's sole authority and exclusive position, we must deal with it. Resentment in our hearts clearly reveals such things. Instead of allowing a root of bitterness to take hold that ultimately could destroy us, we ought to thank the Lord when He brings to light these hidden things. Such resentments taking root are like cockroaches scrambling to hide when the light switch goes on in darkened rooms exposing them. This happens because we can allow crumbs of unsound expectations to lie around the empty caverns of our hearts. We must be vigilant to deep clean these areas so that those offenses can be revealed and purged.

Offenses come easily when we have put an unhealthy expectation on someone to be our provision or expect that person to give us what we need. When they don't come through, offense sets in. But God never desires that kind of relationship with others in the first place. Romans 13:8 makes this very clear:

> *Let no debt remain outstanding, except the continuing debt to love one another, for whoever loves others has fulfilled the law.*

That word "debt" means (among other things), "to be under obligation." We are not to be under obligation, nor hold anyone else hostage to our obligations, especially if they fall short of their agreement so that our love for them is in any way diminished. This does not mean that we should avoid necessary legal contracts in life; that would be impossible. But try to maintain a debt-free relationship with others so no one can hold anything over you and vice-versa.

Living Free and Uncontrolled

Living free is a wonderfully powerful feeling, and it allows us to love people instead of feeling indebted to them or controlled by them. How do people control us? We let them. Nobody has the power to control us, chain us and hold us to something they need us to do. Paul says this:

> *For which I am suffering even to the point of being chained like a criminal. But God's word is not chained.*

2 Timothy 2:9

I love that. Even though he is chained, he is not chained. The word of God in him can't be constrained. I love this famous quote by David Wilkerson in the book, *The Cross and the Switchblade*[1]. In response to Nicky Cruz, the gangster who wanted to kill him, he said:

> Yeah, you could do that. You could cut me up into a thousand pieces and lay them in the street, and every piece will still love you.

What does this mean? You can't control what I do from the inside. You may be able to control me externally with pain, the threat of death, etc., but I will still serve the Lord by walking in love. The three Hebrew young men in the book of Daniel made a similar declaration when they were being challenged to worship the idol of the king or be thrown into a blazing fire.

> *And Nebuchadnezzar said to them, "Is it true, Shadrach, Meshach and Abednego, that you do not serve my gods or worship the image of gold I have set up? Now when you hear the sound of the horn, flute, zither, lyre, harp, pipe and all kinds of music, if you are ready to fall down and worship the image I made, very good. But if you do not worship it, you will be thrown immediately into a blazing furnace. Then what god will be able to rescue you from my hand?" Shadrach, Meshach and Abednego replied to him, "King Nebuchadnezzar, we do not need to defend ourselves before you in this matter. If we are thrown into the blazing furnace, the God we serve is able to save us from it, and he will deliver us from Your Majesty. But even if he does not, we want you to know, Your Majesty, that we will not*

serve your gods or worship the image of gold you have set up."

Daniel 3:14-18

I love it when people can't be stopped from standing up for what they believe, despite the consequences, threat of punishment or even death. That is a person who is truly free of a poverty spirit. The root of poverty has nothing to do with money and everything to do with powerlessness. It is the inability to do something about your circumstances. It is a helplessness that says if only the one who is in charge would look my way, then I would be able to do something. With such a belief system, that impoverished person is chained and powerless.

Growing up, I saw the stress in church leaders about finances. The inadequate tithes of our church, where my father pastored, had become a limitation to what was possible in its growth potential, Kingdom influence and expansion. The tithers and those who did not tithe seemed to hold the keys of power over the destiny of the church. Many leaders try very hard to get more and more people to come to their church, and even harder to get their regular members to give their tithe. They are convinced this will help their church move forward, or at the very least, pay the bills. But, more often than not, this method is just an offense waiting to happen.

When you have anyone in your life who seemingly holds all the cards, this can create the potential for you to become offended by that person or that entity or group of people, if they don't give you what you were expecting to receive from them. Whether verbally communicated or simply understood, you have a specific expectation in mind from that person, and they are supposed to bring *that* into the relationship. The offense results when the expectation of that relationship is unmet. If I, as a member in a congregation expect something from my pastor, or as a staff member or employee I expect something from my leader or boss, but they don't follow through with it, I can become offended. That offense may eventually shut the relationship down and turn the offended person out of the congregation, ministry, or business. Thus, the offended person becomes like an unyielding wall of resistance.

In reality, an offense can become an open door to the enemy or it can become an open door to our destiny, depending on our response towards it. We must choose!

An offended person, however, becomes an easy target for the enemy to pick off and take out of commission. Hebrews 12:15 says:

> *See to it that no one falls short of the grace of God and that no bitter root grows up to cause trouble and defile many.*

We have to watch that the initial frustration, anger, and resentment of unmet expectations doesn't turn us off the course of our destiny and into the ditch of bitterness and self-pity. Note the victim language of an offended person:

- "They failed me . . ."

- "If only he would have done what he said . . ."

- "Why didn't they meet their end of the deal?"

The words "they," "them," and "those people," are clear indications there has been a separation from the community of family and friends with whom these offended ones have been partnering. Whenever the language becomes "them" and "us," we have eaten the root of bitterness down to its core and are well on our way to being taken down. Jesus told a parable to explain what happens to those who refuse to forgive or release those who have offended them:

> *In anger his master handed him over to the jailers to be tortured, until he should pay back all he owed.*

Matthew 18:34

When we don't forgive those who have hurt us, we are then subject to the torturous treatment by the demonic realm and ultimately deposed from our place of authority. The long-term consequences of such actions are serious indeed.

Becoming a Powerful Person

But those who are free of poverty and offense are powerful people. They are unable to be held down when people try to constrain them. People who are powerful are not victims of their circumstances because they recognize that God ultimately can deliver them to a more positive outcome of blessing despite their temporary confines.

In the book of Genesis, we see Joseph, the eleventh son of Jacob, certainly had the opportunity to be offended. He had been severely mistreated by his brothers, sold into slavery, sent far away from his family and homeland, falsely accused by Potiphar's wife, and held unjustly in prison. But notice what the Scriptures say about him.

And he sent a man before them—Joseph, sold as a slave. They bruised his feet with shackles, his neck was put in irons, till what he foretold came to pass, till the word of the LORD proved him true.

Psalm 105:17-19

Joseph was not in the most favorable circumstances for many years. It seemed like his dreams and aspirations of leadership would never come to pass. But Joseph's vision was always calibrated from a greater reality. In the midst of constraints, shackles, and chains, he continued to believe God is good, and that He had a powerful destiny once the word of the Lord freed him from his present injustice.

The Key is Perspective

Here's the key: You may not be able to change your circumstances immediately, but you can change the way you *view* your circumstances. You can look at your circumstances from an earthly perspective and walk in a place of helplessness, or you can choose to view them from a higher perspective—the perspective of one seated in Christ above it all. You can be a person filled with hope and excitement about what God is *about* to release on your behalf.

Some people see the world and what is going on all around and it fills them with hopelessness and fear and dread as they wonder how they'll ever make it in such a dark and God-forsaken place. Others see from Heaven's reality and live with the continual hope of going from glory to glory, fully convinced that God is always good, and that He will demonstrate His nature of goodness through them.

In Isaiah 6, the prophet Isaiah hears the seraphs declaration:

> *Holy, holy, holy is the LORD Almighty; the whole earth is full of his glory.*
>
> v 3

From a heavenly perspective, the only thing the seraphs see is God's glory all around, His goodness, the brilliance of His light, and the advancement of the His Kingdom. According to Ephesians, we, too, have been positioned in heavenly places:

> *And God raised us up with Christ and seated us with him in the heavenly realms in Christ Jesus.*
>
> 2:6

We are commanded in Colossians to maintain this heavenly paradigm:

> *Since, then, you have been raised with Christ, set your hearts on things above, where Christ is, seated at the right hand of God. Set your minds on things above, not on earthly things.*
>
> 3:1-2

It is imperative that we also recognize the position we hold on the frontlines of the battlefield: the high ground. In the old days of war, the "high ground" was coveted. It was the place in which an army held the advantage over their enemy who had to climb *up* to them. From this high vantage point, you could see the enemy coming afar off and prepare for conflict in sufficient time. In the Kingdom, we hold the high ground. Offense comes when we don't recognize that we have the upper hand. The enemy is always attempting to bring us down to his low level to defeat us.

Contending for the Blessing

This does not mean that we hold such a powerful position in the Kingdom to exercise domination over people. Ephesians makes this very clear:

> *Put on the full armor of God, so that you can take your stand against the devil's schemes. For our struggle is not against flesh and blood, but against the rulers, against the authorities, against the powers of this dark world and against the spiritual forces of evil in the heavenly realms.*

6:11-12

Our fight is not against people, nor are we trying to get the upper hand in a situation. Rather, we are each called to rest in the Father's arms and recognize how very good He is, and from that perspective, realize that the whole earth is full of His glory. There is goodness all around for the taking, so there is no reason why every single person on the planet should not prosper. There are enough blessings to go around.

In this place of blessing and glory, Philippians 4:19 declares:

> *And my God will meet all your needs according to the riches of his glory in Christ Jesus.*

That means jobs, money, full provisions, healing, and anything else we need, are all available in His glory. If God could provide for over a million people wandering in the desert forty years—people who had no jobs for income, or gardens to harvest food, or stores to shop in—can't He take care of each one of our needs? Do you believe He has more than enough for each one of us so that we can also be generous with one another? Or do you believe, rather, that there is only just enough to squeak by so that we barely make it through? No, our God is a good and glorious God of abundance who loves to provide generously for His children in ways we have not yet seen or even thought to ask.

Who's Enthroned on Your Heart?

To get us to this place, however, we must be far removed from offense. That place of offense is where we have erringly made someone more powerful in our mind than God. We may have unconsciously believed that these individuals hold the key to our success, and if they don't open the door for us, we won't make it. But God alone wants to hold those keys and that high position. Sometimes it takes an extreme act to set us free of that offensive situation. For me, an extreme act was required; so God Himself revealed my heart's need to trust Him alone as the higher source.

A whole new season had been opened up to me. The offense of not having enough students back home had shown me how I had wrongly put the church, the students, and the leaders as the provider for my finances. My heart's throne had an imposter on it, but by God's grace, it was revealed so it could be thrown off. Getting a revelation of any offense we have in our heart towards someone is just the beginning of coming out of bondage to that person.

35

In the next chapter, we will explore being willing to do what it takes to unhook your heart from having a person, a leader, or a circumstance hold the keys to your destiny. Freedom to dream, to live, and to be all that is in your heart is the result of choosing this path, and it is the path that God desires for every single person.

QUESTIONS TO PONDER

1. Has there been a situation in your life that has revealed you are expecting someone to be your provider other than God? Take a minute to revisit that situation.

_____

_____

_____

_____

_____

2. Have you been, or are you currently, offended at someone or frustrated or angry that they have not held up on their end of a deal to provide for you? What is it revealing about you and your dependence upon God?

_____

_____

_____

_____

_____

3. How could you make an adjustment in your expectations towards that person, organization, or business, where you are holding that offense? What would an adjustment look like?

_____

_____

_____

_____

_____

_____

Two

GOD IS YOUR SOURCE

O ur family came back to the U.S. after those life-changing ten weeks in Fiji to a house in storage and an immediate need for housing. Not only did we face uncertainty with a place to live, but we also returned to our home church undergoing some major shifts. Here I was with a church in transition, an uncertain employment, a shaky house situation, and no credit because of my recent foreclosure.

The Path Out of Poverty

The offense I had towards the situation I was in, the Fijians, and the staff at my church was God's way of helping me to see that my foundation of provision needed major adjusting.

As it turns out, a generous and hospitable couple in our church let us live in a few rooms of their house for several months while we searched for a place to rent. I knew we needed a miracle as we began house-hunting since a renter is required to show a good credit report, sufficient monthly income equal to at least three times the amount of the rent, and a favorable renter's report from the previous houses rented. Well, I had no credit, and only that month did I get an unusually substantial offering, which was enough to show I did have the adequate income needed. Thankfully, our previous realtor also provided a favorable report, stating that we were a "great family and financially reliable." By God's grace, we were able to secure a rental home within a reasonable timeframe. He is so faithful.

Next I had to get my job situation sorted out. We ended up leading several short-term supernatural schools that year as we attempted to create some new synergy with potential students and thereby generate income to cover our living expenses. During this time, the old resentment I had felt for not having enough students from the original school that would have provided for our needs was a nagging irritation. So, I confronted this within myself, and then decided the best thing to do would be to talk it out with our senior leadership team. That helped somewhat, and I was on track again with my living and employment situation stabilized.

Living the Dream

I continued running the schools for the remainder of the year but knew something had to shift for me. I felt I was looking for the church, the students, the leaders, and the salary to be my financial providers. The leaders held a genuine desire to take care of me and even offered to increase my income. But deep down,

I knew there was something greater awaiting. I felt the daily routine of administration was more of a drudgery and not quite what I had expected when I initially dreamed about setting up supernatural schools. I realized I was much better at *establishing* schools than I was at handling the day-to-day pastoral needs of the students and the administration required. I knew I needed to run them for a few years to learn how to facilitate them, but at this point, the grace had lifted. That combination of issues led me to make the decision to resign my job at the end of the school season. I didn't know what I was going to do after I resigned but it was clear to me that God was advancing me into something else and I knew I couldn't stay in the present ministry position. It was necessary for me to release the church, the students, and my leaders from the unreasonable expectation of providing for my needs. Instead I needed to position myself where God alone was my sole source of provision. This would be a huge faith leap for me that I knew I must do.

When I first shared this with my leaders, I didn't put on false airs of someone super-spiritual, nor did I announce that I was planning to just "live off what came from above" or live "by faith." Rather, I explained that I had come to a point in my life that I knew God was up to something and I simply needed to yield to it. I shared the struggle of my offense regarding the very few students registered for the school, and forgave them for the offense I had carried, and then I blessed them for their faithful and generous care of my needs and salary. They, in turn, forgave me, returned their blessing to my family and me, and I was assured of their full support. From that point on, I felt fully free to pursue God in whatever He had for me.

Stepping Out

I immediately stepped into a traveling/preaching ministry that took me to nations far beyond my borders. It took me awhile to recognize it, but this was the best decision I could have made. It was a heart decision to find a place of provision that did not allow one person or one source as my provider. Though people are often a means by which God provides, in this season I needed to establish Him to be the primary source of all provision and to observe how He was carefully watching out for my wellbeing and the wellbeing of my family. The offense had been dealt with as I forgave those for whom I held wrong expectations, and I simply stepped out of the situation that was inciting the offense.

It wasn't too long before I could see that God was up to something *good* and that He was inviting me into a higher way of living. Internally I determined that if He couldn't provide for me through my partnership with Him to steward my resources, then I was done. This was a moment of stepping off the cliff to trust God completely—the moment of no return.

And this was the very moment that changed my life for the good.

Reality Check

So, let me ask you some questions as you consider your present state:

- Is there someone or something in your life with whom you are offended? Could it be a spouse, a son or daughter, a sibling, a friend, pastor, boss, a neighbor, a co-worker or someone who works for you, or a congregation with whom you're in relationship?

- Who are you clinging onto so tightly in hopes that their generosity will benefit you?

- Who are you waiting for to hand you down an inheritance, a blessing, or promotion into a position of advancement? It may be that God Himself wants to promote you, but He is constrained from allowing it until your eyes are solely on Him for your blessing or advancement.

When you look to God for the full resolution and provision for all you need, it frees you up so that you're not focused on trying to control your circumstances and others based out of fear. When we wait for our expectations to come from people, we end up trying to manipulate them because of our fear, our piteous condition, or our dire and most urgent need. Beware. The very nature of that way of living is witchcraft. With such desperate attempts, we try to force God's hand through whiny, self-pity prayers that beg Him to change someone or something in our favor. Instead, we should apply His grace and power, and partner with Him and His gifts to discover Heaven's wisdom and strategy in our situation.

Remember, His ways are always peaceable.

The Path of Hope

I know some of you feel so helplessly bound to your circumstances, economic status, type of job or lack of income, the area you are living in, past or present realities, and so on. But the truth is that none of these things are more powerful than who God is for you. He can lead you out of that seemingly hopeless place into abundance despite the odds you face.

You may feel the conviction of the Lord to release people that you have been holding back. Maybe you are a door opener to help people step into their destiny. Perhaps you have been controlling the resources entrusted to you out of fear, or you're afraid of what releasing people into their destiny might do to your present, carefully-controlled environment. Or you might need to simply walk away from circumstances that have embittered you. The caution in taking such an action, however, is to make sure you are not going to walk into another circumstance where the very same thing is repeated. Sometimes you may need to stay put in your situation but change the perspective on how you view it. God always offers a higher perspective of our vision.

When I stepped out of the salary position, I stepped into trusting God more fully. Over the next several years, I learned the value of keeping God on the throne of provision in my heart. When it was forever settled, God repositioned me back into a part-time salary position, along with other sources of income that I had learned to develop. Now I am free of that debilitating mindset, and I'm living in a much healthier place internally. If at any time the job and the salary starts to restrict the dreams of my heart, I know I have the power to step out of it and that I will find other means of provision. It has placed me in a more powerful position where I now live free at all times. It has allowed me to hold the keys of my destiny with the Lord as the one who leads and guides me. Yes, I am free . . . and with God's help, I will stay free!

A salary is not the issue, by the way; it's your mindset regarding a salary. Ask yourself: *Am I serving this salaried position or is it serving me?* If I am "bowing down" to the salary, so to speak, and to the one who is providing it for me, then it has me. If I am graciously receiving it as a part of God's provision for my life, knowing that He, ultimately, is the one giving this to me as a stream of income, then it is okay.

Sometimes the dangling carrot that holds someone to a way of life, a job, a salary, or even a relationship, is with the hopeful expectation that more will come out of it. Sometimes the only expectation is: *This is it; this is as good as it gets. No use hoping for something better or something more. It's just not there.* If our lifeline imprisons us within predictability—confines that keep us from soaring into our dreams—then that is poverty's hold on us. Such a poverty mindset restricts dreams instead of empowering them by limiting our potential and possibilities. Yet God is always leading us to break out of such a place. You could be a person with millions of dollars and still be constrained by the very money that could launch you into your destiny. The issue is never the amount of money you have but whether that money controls you. Does it enable or disable you? Does it imprison you or set you free to explore your full potential? The answers to these questions should motivate us to make the necessary changes to our freedom.

Heavenly Perspective

Jesus gave a very specific directive to the rich young ruler about his money:

> *Jesus looked at him and loved him. "One thing you lack," he said. "Go, sell everything you have and give to the poor, and you will have treasure in heaven. Then come, follow me."*

Mark 10:21

Some misinterpret this Scripture to mean Jesus wanted to take away all his money, as if He was saying that money is evil. But He was simply addressing the issue of this young man's relationship to his money. He identified that his money had a hold on him and it had become his security. Jesus alone holds that place in our hearts and He will always go after the imposter! He knew this young man wanted to be His disciple, and oh, how He loved him! So He offered him the wonderful opportunity to adjust the heart attachment with his wealth. The benefits and blessings of releasing the grip that money can hold in our life cannot be underestimated. In fact, Jesus went on to tell him about the avalanche of blessings when we reprioritize our attachments to wealth:

> *"Truly I tell you," Jesus replied, "no one who has left home or brothers or sisters or mother or father or children or fields for me and the gospel will fail to receive a hundred times as much in this present age: homes, brothers, sisters, mothers, children and fields—along with persecutions— and in the age to come eternal life."*

Mark 10:29-30

God's primary interest in our lives is to remove that which keeps us from being abundantly blessed. The fact is, He really wanted to give the rich young ruler a hundred-fold *more* than he already had! But first, Jesus needed to make sure his heart was fully surrendered, and that required him giving up what he presently had. Jesus has no problem with people who have great wealth; it is His blessing to them, after all. He is after this one issue: *Is the King first in your life?*

Nations ultimately are going to bow down to Jesus and give Him their wealth as well. Many wars have been fought because people groups are trying to desperately hold onto the security that land and resources provide. When nations see that Jesus is a good provider and has given each nation a generous inheritance of land with valuable resources to steward, develop and trade, then there will be an increasing peace. So much of what is fought over comes out of the fear of lack, and God wants to show us He has provided enough for the entire world.

I've shared here in this chapter the circumstances that led me to step away from a predictable salary into unknown territory. The offense had been dealt with by resigning from my employment position and salary and the predictability that held me captive to it. Invisible hands caught me as I stepped off that cliff of no return and carried me right to a new destiny— that place where I began to recognize my value and discovered hidden resources.

In the next chapter, I want to talk about becoming a resource and the need to recognize that you are worthy of being blessed to access this provision from Heaven.

QUESTIONS TO PONDER

1. Is there a position, job, or individual that immobilized you and kept you from stepping into the person you really are (one who is more powerful and financially free)? Describe that situation.

_____

_____

_____

_____

2. Is there somewhere new you need to step towards that is different than where you are currently (i.e., job, location, position)? Why have you not fully pursued the dream of your heart or moved into greater financial freedom? Describe the hindrances.

_____

_____

_____

_____

3. Have you been waiting for someone to do something for you, hoping for a handout, or expecting a promotion that would lead

to an advancement? Explore what that "waiting" place looks like (i.e., frustration, offense, anger, etc.,) and what it stirs within you.

_____

_____

_____

4. What would it look like if you decided, instead, to trust God to provide everything you desired? Describe that, and include your heart dreams.

_____

_____

_____

5. How would you measure your heart attachment to money? Are you motivated by fear when it comes to finances and wealth? What adjustment can you make to live free financially and be positioned for the flow of abundance from Heaven?

_____

_____

_____

Three

ESTABLISH YOUR VALUE

*V*aluing yourself and knowing what you're worth is a huge step in disengaging from a poverty mindset. In the previous chapters, we discovered that offense often reveals a bondage to a person or even a system that can restrain those held in its grip. In this chapter, we will explore how to enter into a revelation of your incredible value and worth according to Heaven's scale. This is the key to living in perpetual freedom and abundance.

No Honor, No Value

Provision comes to those who know they are valued. For me, experiencing God's provision through an itinerant ministry taught me to value myself. As I stepped out of a regular church staff salary, I stepped into pursuing a new stream of income. It didn't come easy, I can tell you. But I was faithful with what little I received at the beginning, even in times when I received no honor or value in return for my ministry.

When I first launched out on my own, I had not yet received any speaking opportunities, with the exception of one church. A pastor acquaintance I had known for a few years invited me to speak, so I accepted. After an extended period of worship that Sunday morning, a number of long and drawn-out announcements, various ones stepping up to share, the pastor finally introduced me. As I stepped up onto the platform to preach, he signaled that he was giving me only about 10 minutes and emphasized that he needed to end the service by 12:30. I glanced at the clock . . . *It was already 12:20!* Obviously I had anticipated a longer time to share with the congregation, but I honored that 10-minute segment I was given.

We had a potluck following the service, giving an opportunity for everyone to visit for an extended period of time. As I was about to leave, the pastor took me to the gas station to fill up my car for the trip home. But there was no honorarium that day, nor did I feel the honor normally extended to an invited minister. I left a bit stunned. *Sheesh . . .* I thought, *if this keeps up, my family and I could be out on the streets without a roof over our head.* My present situation was a bit uncertain, for sure, and I was fighting the growing anxiety when I really thought about it: I had no credit, no steady income to rely on, no church gas cards to fill up my car when I desperately needed it—none of the usual perks of being salaried. I had nothing but *hope* for what I believed would eventually unfold in my ministry. And it was hope that became my fuel and primary motivator. With this vision before me, I determined to press on through and continue to trust God.

Following that Sunday meeting, I was invited to another church about 7 hours away. I loved this church and the people loved me, but I soon discovered that they, too, didn't have a built-in culture that honored their guests. Though I gave it my all as I preached that Sunday, I left with no offering or honorarium. Now the financial pressure was really beginning to build. Not only was my mind reeling with concern, *What am I going to do to live? . . .* but I was also dealing with the anger at feeling so devalued. *Don't churches know even the basics of how to care for itinerant ministers?* I thought. I had pastored for over ten years and worked hard with what I knew at that time on how to bless the guest speakers we had invited. For the small church we pastored in Willits, I considered us to be very generous. I look back now and realize there were things I didn't think about in caring for our invited speakers, but it was only out of ignorance. But we definitely gave generously out of what we were able to give and always made sure to honor our guests with the full value of their worth!

Setting Your Value

I am going to have a conversation with some pastors, I thought. It seemed fairly obvious to me that a guest speaker should be well taken care of following ministry in their congregation. I certainly wasn't expecting anything extravagant. I just knew I needed to communicate clearly that, at the very least, I should receive a financial offering and should have travel expenses and meals taken care of for that trip. So I began to figure out how I was going to have that conversation with pastors. I think sometimes people just don't realize that ministers who travel for a living, also have a household with bills to pay. While we are out ministering on the road, we still have the normal life stuff concerns, and quite frankly, a token offering of $200 doesn't go very far to take care of a family of four. And if I had a handful of meetings a month, with such a small offering, I would very quickly be in big financial trouble.

Figuring out how to share my needs was quite a challenge for me. It's like asking for a raise at work. My mind was reeling with questions, *What if they say, 'No, we can't do that . . .'? Then I'd run the risk of having no speaking engagement at all!* . . . and that caused great anxiety within me. But, another question I asked myself was, *Am I valuable enough that they would want to pay for me to come?* So many thoughts like these were racing through my head. *As an itinerant ministry, this is my job! And just like someone with a specialty job skill, it has a value . . . high value, in fact. . . . I know I am worth paying.* The fear of rejection was keeping me from what I knew was Heaven's payscale linked with my value. But God gave me courage to push through my fears so that His value on my life and ministry would be well established in me. This is what I knew I had to communicate to pastors and ministry leaders.

So with fear and trembling, I decided to share this with a pastor who was inviting me back to speak at his church a second time. I didn't feel bold enough talk to him directly on the phone. Instead I wrote an email that stated, "I'd love to come to minister to your church. I need to ask for an honorarium, plus extra to cover my gas and meal expenses . . ."

He sent back a reply asking, "How much do you need to come to our church?" I took some time to think about this because I had to figure out what my specific needs were and what I would need to be financially remunerated to where it was worth the trip. *What would be an amount that I could feel good about asking?* I estimated a reasonable amount and sent this back to him. *It seems to be a fair offering*, I thought. *I am only asking to cover my basic essentials*. But even still, it was way outside my comfort zone to *ask* for it. It seemed to take a long time to hear back from him, but the pastor finally replied with, "We can do that."

What a relief! *He agreed to give what I asked for!* For me, this was an important start at setting a value on my work and ministry.

So now I would like to ask you to consider the following questions as you evaluate your own work—whatever it is—and value:

- How much are you worth?

- Where do you need a raise?

- How would you initiate the conversation with your boss/employer about needing a raise?

- What are the fears you face in thinking about asking for a raise?

- Did you ask for a raise? How did it turn out?

- Have you asked for one before and it didn't turn out well? What were the emotions you felt about being turned down? Did it make you angry? Did you get fired-up inside? Did you go after a new job?

- In thinking about a raise, what is the amount God is telling you that you are worth?

- Is it time for you to talk about this with your boss or just keep it between you and God?

Where Blessings Flow

Let me share a brief side note here. We all have our own views about the right way to go about acquiring money, especially as it relates to ministers and Christian ministry. The one thing I have learned is not to judge how others receive their provision. When we judge someone else, we open ourselves up to a spirit of judgment, which shuts down our blessing. Our main focus is knowing what is right according to the Word of God and being confident in how He is leading us specifically into financial provision and prosperity. His leading is very personal—between the person and the Lord. We also know that each person will be accountable to God for how they steward His financial blessings. But ultimately, we cannot live under another person's convictions about how we receive financial provision, and likewise, we should not judge how others manage and steward their finances.

The Way of Love

At this point in my itinerant ministry, unpaid bills were beginning to pile up and my rent was late. I didn't want to push the favor I had with the owner of our house who had already allowed me to rent without a good credit report. I have heard it said that there are two motivators: pain or pleasure. The pain of late bills was definitely driving my desire to get into a better financial place and to figure out this new way of life as an itinerant on the road. I had always loved calling pastors, preaching in churches, and being around God's people, but to *have* to call pastors because I needed meetings to meet financial obligations made me feel like a cheap salesman. It greatly affected my normal jovial, confident self in conversations with other ministers because I *needed* something from them.

The interesting result in that season was that when I was desperate to secure a meeting to get money to pay the bills, I received no invitations! But when I just opened my heart up to loving on a person and nurtured friendship like I've always enjoyed, a door or two opened up. Gratefully, I took up their offer and carefully pursued their trust. And slowly, ever so slowly, more doors started to open.

I had spent ten years building some great connections with key fathers and mothers in the revival movement that I loved and readily embraced. I never thought these would be the ones to open doors and make the way for me. I had always embraced them as life mentors, ones who really helped me in my development. Graciously, a few of them offered a few preaching opportunities where they were unable to attend. One of them knew I was a solid prophetic voice and so he sent me a few pastors to contact and offer a prophetic word for them. A few doors opened as a result, but more importantly, I was developing a real *heart* for these leaders while at the same time being very careful not to relay my pressing financial needs. I prophesied over many leaders through a variety of means, and occasionally, that connection turned out to be really valuable. Through all of this, I was learning something significant: **I am valuable.** I was also learning that my prophetic gifts could open doors, but that my heart had to be right so as not to prostitute my gifts in hopes of future profitable opportunities. Learning that delicate balance was key.

An Impoverished King

The very meaning of the word "poverty" in the Book of Daniel has to do with a lack of valuing oneself. Daniel had been given the task of interpreting Nebuchadnezzar's dream for him. It was a pretty terrifying dream and its interpretation referred to

Nebuchadnezzar's authority being stripped away from him until he acknowledged the Lord as the only one who elevates leaders. Daniel then gave him a piece of advice so as to avert potential judgment from heaven.

> *Wherefore, O king, let my counsel be acceptable unto thee, and break off thy sins by righteousness, and thine iniquities by shewing mercy to the poor; if it may be a lengthening of thy tranquility.*
>
> Daniel 4:27, KJV

Daniel instructed the king to be kind to the poor, or, "the oppressed", as it says in the NIV, in order to avoid judgment. That word "poor"[2] is very interesting in the ancient Semitic language of Aramaic and underscores our study here. The Aramaic word means, "to self-abase, chasten or punish yourself", and "be hard on yourself". That is very descriptive of poor people and those who carry a poverty spirit. The very nature of a poverty spirit is that the people do not value themselves. Those under this spirit are so hard on themselves because they don't think they are enough and believe that what they do have to offer isn't valuable. So they ask themselves, *Do people* really *want what I have?*

Journey Out of a Poverty Mindset

I remember watching the British TV show, "Britain's Got Talent". In one of the episodes, there was a featured contestant named, Paul Potts. At his very first performance, he timidly stood centerstage wearing a pretty shabby suit. Waiting for the music to cue up, he didn't look all that impressive and you could tell by his posture that he had very little confidence. But when he opened his mouth and began to sing, this amazing big voice came out of him. He stunned the audience with his rich operatic voice. Come to find out, he was just a phone company salesman, a real simple guy. But through the journey of subsequent performances within the series that year, Paul's value, self-esteem, and courage dramatically improved. By the end of the season, his countenance, confidence, and outward demeanor had transformed so significantly, he ended up winning. Clearly, as his own value was raised, his true identity emerged that shifted everything for him.

The journey that the Lord had me on was to break poverty off of my life. I was on track for the big win. But first I had to recognize that God had put something highly **valuable** inside of me that required a broader region for influence. The prophetic, the heart of worship, the preaching, the breaker anointing, signs and wonders, and the equipping call, were all there inside of me. I didn't realize how amazing all those things were and that God wanted to use these to open His Body up to greater expressions of His glory through them. I learned that I don't get to determine the level of influence God has assigned to me, but I am responsible to step into releasing who I am, and that I must do it without hesitation or any shred of a lack of confidence in order to see the full measure God desires for each of those gifts.

The very nature of poverty is to be extremely hard on yourself. You never think you are good enough. It doesn't matter how good you do; you always strive to improve. I love improving for the sake of excellence, but so often we seek to improve for the sake of perfectionism. We don't think we are good enough just as we are, and as a result, we often overanalyze every single thing we do. I can remember many years of coming home from preaching or leading worship and going into a period of introspection over the events of the day and my performance. I would begin to nitpick every single thing that I had just done:

You missed it right there, Keith . . . You should have sung that song earlier, Keith. Why didn't you stop preaching then, Keith? It would have been so much more impactful if you had only done that. You said way too much there . . . On and on and on the introspection merry-go-round would go until I would be sick . . .

But still, I just couldn't seem to find my way off that cyclical spin of self-criticism.

Fast to Break Poverty Thoughts

One day the Lord said to me, "Keith, I want you to go on a fast. I want you to fast introspection. For the next 30 days, I don't want you to think one negative thought about yourself. I don't want you to be hard on yourself or evaluate one single thing. Only kind thoughts about yourself will be allowed."

I thought to myself, *Lord, there is no way I can make it through to 30 days. Well, it's possible I might make it 30, but on day 31, I just know I am going to be hard on myself again.* Those were my honest thoughts.

But I went on that fast just as the Lord instructed. How painful it was, too, but how incredibly freeing it was to have the loving directive of the Father to simply think wonderful things about myself. I had His personal permission not to be hard on myself and to only think the best thoughts possible. Wow. Every thought that came across the screen of my brain was tested by whether or not it was uplifting. That was a first.

Now I know there are times when God wants to correct something in our lives that needs an upgrade. However, in this season, I was learning that if He wanted to talk about something that needed adjustment, He would bring it specifically to my attention. Meanwhile, I would only be allowed to think good thoughts about myself, and He could correct me when needed concerning wrong thoughts or behaviors. But unless He spoke up, I would only think good thoughts.

Philippians 4:8 became my model for this retraining:

> *Finally, brothers and sisters, whatever is true, whatever is noble, whatever is right, whatever is pure, whatever is lovely, whatever is admirable— if anything is excellent or praiseworthy—think about such things.*

Sometimes we have such a harsh view of ourselves. And yet, the ability to flourish and prosper comes as a result of believing that you are a wonderful person with something valuable to contribute. Consider this: You are made in the image of God, and He actually *likes* you! Psalm 139 reveals that His thoughts for you outnumber the sands of the seashore.

> *How precious to me are your thoughts, God! How vast is the sum of them! Were I to count them, they would outnumber the grains of sand—when I awake, I am still with you.*
>
> 17-18

With only good thoughts toward us, Jeremiah 29:11 tells how God plans for our prosperity.

> *"For I know the plans I have for you," declares the LORD, plans to prosper you and not to harm you, plans to give you hope and a future."*

These and other Scriptures speak of how much God values us. The thoughts we think about ourselves should be patterned in the same way as God's are toward us.

A New View of You

The Lord shared another view about who I am in Christ. He asked me, "Are you a new creation?"

"Yes, Lord," I replied.

"Doesn't that mean that Christ lives inside of you?" He asked.

"Yes, Lord," I replied once again.

He went on, "And, so it's not you that lives now but it is Christ who lives in you, correct?"

"Yes, Lord."

He continued, "Is Jesus sitting on His throne being harsh with Himself?"

I thought, *No . . .*

"Is Jesus beating Himself up thinking, *You should have done more today. You should have prayed harder, given more, been better at that . . .* ?"

Of course not! came my immediate thought.

Then He said, "You are in Christ. *You* no longer live . . . Christ lives *in* you. Jesus is *never* having a bad day. He is never hard on Himself. And since Christ is your all in all, you shouldn't be harsh on yourself either. Keith, introspection can no longer be allowed in your life."

Boom! Broken! The relief I felt was tangible. *Thank You, Lord, for that revelation!*

But walking this revelation out can be extremely challenging when you've been used to beating yourself up regularly. Who needs a devil to accuse you when you are so good at doing it yourself? It makes it so much easier for the devil when you partner with him in accusing yourself, being harsh with yourself, overanalyzing everything you do, not extending mercy to yourself, or not believing in yourself. What you're really doing is devaluing the very person you are and devaluing your ministry that you offer to the Lord! The enemy loves to fuel your negative emotions and thoughts, and fan those fires of condemnation, guilt, and shame into a blaze about how you could have done better. Don't do it.

Hearing the Father's voice about your value to Him and how He positioned you in Christ will break the enemy's cycle for good. You must determine that this will be the only view of yourself allowed. Retrain your brain to think about yourself like Jesus does.

Recognize Your Value

Becoming a resource to the Body and learning how to present myself before pastors and leaders in a Kingdom-minded way would require that I think about myself differently. It is one thing to get a door open to speak, but it is entirely another to not sabotage that opportunity on the other side. As I've heard some say, "Your gift makes room for you, but your character will keep you where your gift opened the door."

The Lord told me; "Keith the reason you are so intimidated with other leaders is because you don't see yourself as valuable." When you recognize you are valuable, you will carry yourself much differently. Valuable people attract valuable people; poverty-minded people attract the same. Birds of a feather do flock together. If you want to become an influencer, you must walk in your identity as a valuable person, and great influencers will be attracted to that which is inside of you. I know my gifts open doors to great leaders, and to have a well-established mindset where I was comfortable with myself assured that I wouldn't sabotage the favor my gifts brought me.

In light of this, ask yourself these questions:

- What do you think about yourself?

- Are your thoughts frequently about yourself as victorious or are they mostly self-abasing?

- Name ten things about yourself you like.

- List ten things about yourself you would like to change.

- What does God think about the areas that you don't like about yourself? Ask Him.

- Are you willing to fast for a month from negative thinking? List the kind of thoughts you need to spend fasting.

How do you learn your value and break self-abasement thinking? You must learn to listen to who the Lord says you are, and then believe it! The Lord told me once that if I have Him—the King of the universe as my friend—then I would have the kings of the world as my friends as well. If I put my energy into allowing the King of kings to love on me, to speak into my destiny, and listen to and believe His thoughts for me, then I would begin to recognize my worth. God knows His own immeasurable worth, and He created me in His image. That's incredible. Meditate on *that*.

Grow in Favor

You must grow in favor with God and man. I think it is pretty amazing that Jesus had to grow in favor, even though He Himself was God.

> *And Jesus grew in wisdom and stature, and in favor with God and man.*
>
> Luke 2:52

If Jesus had to, then certainly we need to. How do you grow in influence and favor? Well, as I said before, if you make the King of kings your friend, you'll eventually have the kings of the earth and influencers in your life working to help open doors for you. You won't have to manipulate, walk in self-pity, beg, grovel, or any such thing. Doors will fling open for you. Favor does that.

King David is a good example of this. While still a shepherd boy, he grew in favor with the Lord. The Lord found him as a lowly shepherd boy before he was popular with man and certainly before he had any favor with his family. But God found David as a man after His own heart and selected him to be king because his worshiper's heart and love for God was like none other. His lifestyle of worship caused him to be anointed king by the head prophet Samuel in front of his mocking brothers. That anointing caused him to become the king's minstrel, driving away the harassing demons that tormented King Saul as he merely sang and played his instrument. David's heart of worship and favor with God caused him to take out Goliath. His victory over Goliath gave him more favor with man, which enabled him to lead a company of warriors from the armies of Israel, and on and on his favor with God and man grew until eventually, he was elevated as the king of Israel.

The favor of God and man will always lead to the highest positions possible, those necessary for your destiny to be fulfilled.

Establish Kingdom Foundations

Hang around the King, the only one who holds the position of highest value, and let some of what He thinks about you rub off on how you think about yourself. Begin to allow the presence of Jesus penetrate every part of you so that you excel in every task, in your giftings, your callings, and dreams realized. Then continue to faithfully steward the gifts that are bringing you to the next level of destiny in your life. Keep the purity and passion alive for God and watch as He promotes you to greater and greater levels of influence in your world. It may not always be as you expect. Not everyone is meant to be on the platform in front of masses of people. Influence and favor look differently for each of us but is available to all. Like an inheritance stored safely away in a bank deposit box, we must learn how to access it.

In the next chapter, I want to continue to delve into becoming a resource and how to expand the gifts, favor, and destiny on your life until it begins to multiply into a place of great abundance for you.

QUESTIONS TO PONDER

1. Who are the influencers in your world that you greatly admire and look up to?

_____

_____

2. Do you see yourself as an influencer or someone who is inferior to those influencers?

_____

_____

3. How can you posture yourself differently around influencers?

_____

_____

4. What is the wrong way to move into influencer circles? What is the right way?

_____

_____

5. Do you value yourself and see yourself as God sees you?
What does that look like?

_____

_____

6. Do you speak kindly to yourself and build yourself up
even when you make mistakes? If not, how could you make
adjustments?

_____

_____

7. What should you declare over yourself the next few weeks to
begin to agree with how God sees you? Write out that declaration
here.

_____

_____

_____

_____

_____

_____

_____

Four

BECOME A RESOURCE

What the traveling itinerant minister receives in offerings isn't enough to live on most times, even for a very modest lifestyle. Because of this, I began to consider other ways to supplement this income. In recent years, I have had the privilege of being in a resource church with other traveling ministers who have years of experience in this area. The leaders shared with me that developing product to carry with me would create other streams of income, and that this was important to sustain ministry. By doing this, I would not be dependent upon an offering as the only means of income, and I would also be able to offer a product that would benefit the people I ministered to.

So, I began the journey of becoming a resource to the Body.

I put out a music CD and a few preaching CDs. They were pretty simple projects with a low budget, but at least it was a start!

The Value of Your Resource

The challenge for me with having product was that I had to market it when I spoke at a church. But you can't genuinely market something if you don't believe in yourself, so it was tough for me. When I considered advertising my product, I was filled with images of dishonest moneychangers in the house of God. I certainly didn't want to be associated with such people. By contrast, I have trustworthy friends who carry product with them and I began to appreciate how it would really help financially. But the whole concept was definitely awkward for me!

Many thoughts raced through my head as I attempted to present my products publicly: *This sounds so fake . . . seems like I'm doing this just to get their money!* I knew truthfully it wasn't. Yes, I needed the sales revenue, but I also knew the products I offered would be a blessing and that it held God's anointing. When I began to focus on the results it would bring because the messages and songs were God-breathed, I relaxed knowing that people would sincerely benefit from the items I offered.

A Little Help from my Friends

Becoming a resource meant developing product that would benefit others. But oftentimes, you just don't know how to begin. It's always good to turn to your friends who have this experience and brainstorm with them. They know your talents and skills and will often present some solid ideas. My friend, Dan McCollam, is one of those who walked me through the whole process and produced my first music CD. It's amazing when I look back at how small of a project it was, but what a huge task it seemed at the time. Learning how to take what God has given you and turn it into something tangible requires a whole new skill set—a big learning curve for sure, and not for the faint of heart. How thankful I was to *finally* get my very first CD completed!

At the time I made my CD, I didn't have any surplus funds, so Dano graciously produced it, utilizing his terrific musical skills at no charge, and then purchased the first hundred CDs for me to sell! That was such a huge blessing to me, and I was so very, very grateful. Becoming a resource often requires the help of generous friends, and such a kind act can be a great encouragement and communicate how others see your potential. It says: "I believe in you."

True Humility

Being a resource will require that you walk through open doors, take on new skills, and gratefully acknowledge every small step forward as a huge blessing from God. When I first started to break through the mindset of poverty into being a resource, every effort to that end seemed enormous. At times I felt unworthy with such generous help, and so I came across with an overly gushing gratitude. I mean, when we first begin an endeavor, we are often quite dependent on the favor, generosity and knowledge of other people. And how grateful we are for friends we can depend on! But at the same time, inordinate expressions of gratitude can sometimes reflect a lack of understanding about your own worthiness to receive God's blessings; you can get stuck in a deep sense of *un*worthiness. Don't misunderstand me; I believe in showing people how grateful I am for what they do for me. Demonstrating thankfulness is *true* humility, whereas an overemphasis, almost syrupy expressions of gratitude is *false* humility and reveals how unworthy you feel about generosity extended to you. We haven't yet learned how valuable we truly are. For instance, someone receives help from a person of influence, but they can't stop expressing their thanks: "Thank you . . . oh thank you. I'm so grateful. You didn't have to . . . thank you sooooo much." They do this because they haven't learned to appreciate that they, too, are deemed worthy of acts of kindness, care, and generosity. They don't yet see themselves as a person who also has God-given influence. I think, too, it sometimes can reveal an underlying fear, that if we don't go overboard in gratitude, the person may back out of the task we really need them to do. I'll say it again: *Demonstrating inordinate gratitude beyond what are normal expressions reveals that you don't yet believe you are valuable.* We need the wisdom of the Lord to express heart-felt gratitude in all sincerity and true humility. This is something God will go after in our lives.

Bread and Seed

After my first CD came out, another worship CD was produced, and then about ten of my preaching CDs followed. Each CD was a lot of work to produce. I started out with very simple white covers and the title, but then upgraded the packaging to a more colorful and contemporary design. I was striving for excellence with each succeeding project, and I enjoyed it.

Each new product required money, of course. The first couple years of reproducing CDs I bought reproduction equipment in order to sell them. This was before I decided to mass produce them. Each step seemed like another hurdle to get over. As I sold CDs, I then had to reinvest the money towards purchasing more CDs. At that time, I could not "eat" my seed money, because it needed to continually be sown. The challenge is when you need money, you have to *have* money to make money. So, every bit of money that came in, we desperately needed it for living expenses, but had to use some of it to reproduce more products.

Then there was my first book. That was a daunting task that took six years, three editors, thousands of dollars (which I really needed to live on!), and much blood, sweat, and tears. The first four years, I paid $3,000 to an editor that just couldn't seem to get the job done. When I finally presented the book to several writers and publishers, they said that it was good content but not well written. I was devastated! For one, $3,000 was a lot of money for me at the time and I was extremely disappointed and frustrated that it would have to be completely rewritten. At that point, I had only paid $2,000 to the editor and didn't want to pay the last $1,000 because I felt I didn't get what I had expected. I finally did pay the last $1,000, however, but with bitterness in my heart. *That is my hard worked-for money, after all,* I said to myself. I felt like it was all wasted. So I decided to look at it as an important part of my learning experience, to do *all* things well and with honest integrity no matter the personal cost. After all, doing things the right way was more important than just getting the job done.

Establishing Good Foundations

It took awhile for me to get the right perspective on this fouled-up book project. Several of my friends said, "Keith, the first book has to be done right. Take the time to make it excellent because publishing your first book is a big deal. If its poorly written and you publish it anyway just to get it out there, then it will be a reflection of you and your writing. You don't want that." I knew they were right, but realized I was going to have to take *more time* to correct it.

Part of becoming a resource is approaching each task with excellence. The challenge to do that, though, can be costly, and at the beginning stages of my resource development, every bit of money spent was money that was needed for something else.

But this process is so important, and we have to remember that God is faithful to provide all we need.

I finally found another editor who donated her precious time by spending a year with me going line by line to rewrite the book. Every meeting taxed my mental capabilities because I was not used to such detailed thinking. All of these experiences were growth opportunities that further developed my skills and led me down the path of becoming a resource.

Finally, the rewrite of my first book met the approval of several friends who are authors and I sent it off to be formatted for print production. It took months getting through this process, which included the cover design, the final edit, page layouts, etc. Several thousand dollars and another year later, my book was finally ready for print. The whole process of my first book was probably a $7,000 venture . . . a lot of money for me at that time in my life! But the lessons through it all with its valuable learning experience and the end result was definitely worth it!

I have come to realize that although things seem small at the beginning, they are the foundation upon which everything else is built. I remember talking to my friend, Georgian Banov, who was recounting to me how his own ministry got started. He told me, "Keith, as things began to grow in my ministry, I could see ahead what it would look like." Georgian has a successful and fruitful ministry and travels globally more than any person I know bringing the message of the cross and the joy of Heaven right along with it.

He gave me some great advice at that time: "Don't get big too quick! Make sure with every step that you take time to build solid relationships with people. There's great benefit in really getting to know pastors and ministry leaders along the way. As you get to know them and become a good steward of those relationships, then more will be added."

That was wise counsel from Heaven through Georgian, and I believe another aspect of what this Scripture meant:

> *And Jesus grew in wisdom and stature, and in favor with God and* ***man.***
>
> Luke 2:52, emphasis added

Our focus is often on favor with God but we must also appreciate the value of growing in favor with people. I am confident that the good relationships I build now will be a welcome strength in the long term.

Stewarding Valuable Relationships

An individual can grow in favor with people only to the measure that he is a good steward of his relationships. As you care for a person by being his friend and seek to do well for him through the use of your gift, your favor grows. At some point, he may recommend you to someone he knows. Your friend will talk about your character, your skills, and your giftings, and then that person will want to connect with you. Perhaps he has never had you in his church, but heard about you from someone else who had you minister in theirs, and that person spoke favorably about the way you ministered and how they appreciated the spiritual gift(s) you brought, etc. God will always build your favor with men in this way as you nurture others generously with the gifts He has given you.

I don't know how many times I have had a pastor ask me about someone I know in vocational ministry. What I think about that person influences their decision to host them. I have been able to open a good number of doors for other voices because they have personally impacted me. That's the value of stewarding and nurturing your relationships and making sure your character and everything you do is with excellence.

On the other hand, I have also felt compelled to speak a word of caution to a pastor regarding someone when asked specifically about an area in which that person has not yet matured or developed. I am not judging that person's ministry, but only answering the ministry leader truthfully. Sometimes a pastor is looking for a specific type of person with matured gifts who will best minister in his church. With that said, it causes me to always want to put forth my very best in character and giftings as I minister—no matter where I am.

What Kind of Resource are You?

Becoming a resource is multifaceted. It is learning what the resources are that you have to offer. Are you a prophetic voice, a business consultant, a website builder, an encourager, a skilled laborer, creatively talented, a life or fitness coach, or a good manager? There are many different gifts and skills that a resource person has and you must first recognize what those are. So ask yourself what others have told you that they appreciate about you. In what area do people typically compliment you? What expertise do you possess? For instance, if I need my house cleaned and want to hire someone, I want to know that the person cleaning my house does it expertly and so I will ask for recommendations. If someone has used a particular housecleaner and appreciates their attention to detail, then I take their word of recommendation, and that word opens the door for them into my house. That is favor. Likewise if a person has an unfavorable reference from someone I trust, then that may hinder his or her ability to grow in influence with me.

For example, when I moved to Vacaville, I needed to get my piano tuned. I called a guy using the phonebook, and quite honestly, he did a terrible job. Then I contacted a local musician I know who has had his pianos tuned many times. He recommended someone, and they have been my piano tuner ever since. Why? Because they do an amazing job—quickly and efficiently—exactly as I expect. I have now given their name out to other people as someone I recommend as an excellent piano tuner. That's how it works.

Becoming a resource is something everyone is meant to be. You start by identifying your resource, and then asking yourself, *What is it that I can bring to the table?* Whatever it is, it must be quality work that's dependable and reliable. Sometimes people are waiting for the big break and think that when they get there, that's when they start doing their best job. They fail to realize that being faithful in the little things, working every job—no matter how small or insignificant—as skillfully as they possibly can, is what paves the way for future opportunities and greater influence.

Par Excellence

I've seen people get locked into a victim mentality: *If only people would recognize me . . . If only my boss would notice . . . If only I would get a lucky break . . . If only . . . If only . . .* That's not the way to progress. You need to recognize and declare over yourself that you are already a powerful resource with what God has given you and that many open doors are coming your way. Know you are valuable, that favor goes before you, and that you are a much-needed resource in your world. It doesn't matter if it is a current reality or not. You have to speak it out as though it already is, even if it is not yet realized.

I can't stress enough how important it is to do everything with excellence. It is the evidence of God's favor on your life, but we still have to partner with Him, work at it, and go deeper.

Joseph was known for his excellence in everything he did and it stirred up trouble all around him. His brothers hated him because of the favored position he held with their father, his gifted business sense, and the prophetic dreams he had. Joseph needed to learn wisdom on how to share his dreams, and that came over time. In an effort to rid themselves of Joseph and to show their utter disdain for him, his brothers sold him off to a traveling camel caravan of traders en route to Egypt. But shortly thereafter, God promoted Joseph to Potiphar's house. He again proved his usefulness so that Potiphar entrusted his entire household into his capable management. Joseph's well-ordered administration made things so easy and prosperous for Potiphar that he didn't have to concern himself about anything. Joseph managed it all! But once again, he was mistreated, unjustly accused and thrown into prison. Even there his gift made room for him, so that very shortly, he was promoted as overseer of the inmates by the prison guard.

Joseph's leadership and administration gift functioned at a very high capacity as it had been developed over years of working for his father, for Potiphar, and the prison guard. While in prison, his dream interpretation gift kicked in and he provided interpretations for two men from Pharaoh's staff. These proved true, and eventually, that gift brought him before Pharaoh himself, one of the most powerful rulers of the entire region. Following his accurate and astounding interpretation of Pharaoh's dream, Joseph was then promoted to second-in-command over all of Egypt in one swift moment. His gift of administration had been so well executed and stewarded, that when the time came for him to stand before a king, he presented not only the interpretation of Pharaoh's dream, but he also presented wisdom from Heaven on how to implement and administer the *solutions* needed within that interpretation. His well-exercised gift was ready at the most critical moment of history because he had valued each and every opportunity God gave him along the way to bless someone with that gift—even in the midst of rejection, injustice, and a dark, depressing prison. He didn't give in to his pitiful conditions, but instead demonstrated a well-developed gift, which manifested its full maturity through God's favor.

If you want to see promotion, do what you are doing right now with even more excellence. Make it your goal to always work at increasing your skill in order to improve and upgrade your abilities with every task you're given. Don't ever settle for what you already know or shy away from something because it seems too difficult. Push yourself to do what seems impossible for you and then find the way to do it. In this way, you make sure that what you are doing in this present moment has a place to grow and that you'll always be progressing beyond where you are.

Sometimes people feel stuck in a 9-5 job with virtually no potential to utilize or improve their skills and competency. They may have a desire to do so, but their job doesn't fully appropriate their gifts and skills and therefore becomes a dead end. There's nothing to develop or increase, and favor within your realm of influence always requires a place to grow. In the example of Joseph, we see that God continued to break him out of his present sphere—however difficult it was—into the largest arena possible where his influence for the Kingdom had the maximum effect with exponential results.

For someone who desires to break out of their current place and move into a new sphere, I have learned that it is best to develop and discover new ground while continuing in your current sphere. For instance, if I decided I wanted to try pro golf instead of preaching, teaching, leading worship, releasing the prophetic, building supernatural schools, and working with churches and business people, the favor I've known within these realms would not be there. I think I potentially *could* be a good golfer if I really invested my time and energy into it, but I don't personally possess the high-level skills required. For me, that is an arena that is not going to accelerate my influence and will only serve to frustrate me. You may have a dream in a different sphere of influence than where you are, but it's best to ease into it and do some exploration on the side, all while maintaining your present place of favor. When God is ready to move you, it will be clearly evident.

Well-Planted to Flourish

My first job as a teenager was at McDonald's. I really enjoyed that job for the nine months I worked there. It was a good experience for a young teen, but it wouldn't be a good place for my gifts to grow now. If I had continued in that job for the next ten years, maybe I could have worked my way up a few ranks, but the future for me personally would have maxed out pretty quick. You have to know when a place is no longer the best use of your gifts and resources. That's why it's a good idea to assess your present situation from time to time to evaluate how God is leading you forward to mature and utilize your gifts, favor and influence.

Now I know there are seasons when working a job is necessary and needful to pay the bills. That's fine. But it is also needful to make sure there is a place where your gifts will grow and flourish. Where is your outlet that doesn't have a lid? Sometimes your job, ministry, or whatever situation you are currently in can only take you so far. That is good when you are in a season of assignment. Sometimes you are in a certain place for a period of time to teach you some really valid lessons that will contribute to your maturity, but then once it's completed, you get the permission of the Father to pursue your dreams.

Ten years of pastoring in Willits was a season of assignment for me. God was teaching me how to love people well, build a Kingdom wineskin in a church setting, get some relational issues worked on, develop my passion for His presence, expand the prophetic, and build relationships in the region. It was a season God was adding to my foundation much-needed character and gifting to sustain me for my dream season. But once that was done, I received the green light to go! One day, the dream of my heart came up in a conversation with Dano, and it started me on a whole new journey. That journey would require moving to a new location because where I was living at the time had taken me as far as I could go. I knew God was about to activate my giftings to a whole new level where it would be more far reaching—traveling to the nations, expanded teaching and preaching opportunities, resourcing what God had given me, etc. I love the little town of Willits and believe it is an amazing place. But for me, Vacaville became a place that would take the lid off my giftings and help me develop into becoming a resource for the nations. Now could I have done that in Willits? Possibly . . . but probably not. At this point in my life I needed to associate regularly with like-minded leaders who had already walked this path, and I needed to physically reside within an environment that was conducive to developing the kind of skills needed to become a resource.

As you are discovering what kind of resources you have, you also should consider where you need to be planted in order to flourish. You don't need more than one opportunity for your gifting to start working for you. All it takes is one door, one connection, or one relationship to get you started. Sometimes in your season of assignment, you might have to be a good steward of that one opportunity for awhile before it turns into another opportunity. The main objective as you are stewarding that opportunity is to determine if it is a one-time opportunity, an open door, or a connection relationship that has the potential to develop you into another level of favor, influence, and breakthrough in your resource.

Sometimes people have wishful thinking. They stay put in one area hoping someday to get the big break, but that kind of thinking is not correct. Big breaks don't normally come in one moment. It is usually through a series of small steps that leads up to that one moment that people refer to as a big break. Your faithfulness with the small and seemingly insignificant moments enables you to handle the big one when it comes along. Most of the time when someone gets a big break that they weren't prepared for, they sometimes fold under the pressure of that increased favor, because they haven't matured sufficiently to be able to handle the quick rise in favor.

Ready For a Promotion?

The goal in all of this is, like Joseph, to be able to develop no matter what season you are in, to utilize your gift, and to recognize whether you are in a season of assignments or in pursuit of your dreams. How you can distinguish that is by the character you possess. Are you able to handle whatever pressure a full release of your gifting would bring? An honest answer will settle any impatience to move quickly from you where you are and will instead help you learn to be content in your present state while remaining hopeful for the next season where He is leading.

For instance, if you have a housecleaning business and you have been doing one job a week successfully, but you're antsy to increase your business, could you handle it if suddenly you were given jobs that require you to clean several large office buildings? Do you think it would be wise to promote you suddenly from that small job to a very large job? We could crunch the numbers and say that it would definitely be a financial boost, but have you developed the needed leadership skills to manage the increased number of hired employees required to keep your business going? Have you acquired the skills necessary to administer such an enterprise? Maybe you are ready for it. If so, great! Go for it. Maybe you have the skills, the resources, and in this moment you believe you're ready for your big break—just like Joseph's big promotion from the prison to the palace. But remember, this was a position he had prepared for with years of excellent stewardship of his giftings and character, often at a great personal cost and under extreme circumstances. On the other hand, perhaps it would be better to grow your business one client at a time—slowly building it up over time. As you do a great job for one person, they may recommend you to another, then another, and so on. As you develop relationships and rapport with each client by performing an excellent job, your influence grows, your reputation improves, and so does the capacity to handle the next level of business growth.

Prepare for Rain while the Sun is Shining

God wants to prosper each and every one of us and so He's given us gifts, talents, and resources to succeed and flourish in life. As I've said already, sometimes the best way to develop resources that are not yet capable of sustaining you financially is to develop them on the side while still working your other job. Some people don't think about developing other streams of income as long as the one they are in is working. Many times, people are just going along and making it, sometimes they are doing well, but sometimes they are barely getting by. It isn't until the rug is pulled out from under them that they are suddenly forced to develop other resources. That is a very difficult curve in the road to handle. I learned that very quickly as I stepped into becoming an itinerant minister and also worked feverishly at developing myself to be a resource person to the Body. I was very inexperienced. The only factor that drove me day in and day out was the fact that I could potentially be thrown out on the street with my family if I didn't get my bills paid that month! My fear of not having enough financially was all the motivation I needed to keep at it and work hard.

You know a change is coming because you feel bored at what you do. You might even get a hint that things are about to change because you feel the grace is running out where you are. Or maybe your passion is starting to grow in another area to such a degree that in your present work environment, it is hard to stay focused. That may be an indicator that the grace is lifting for where you are presently. You have to make sure you are not trying to get away from what God is training you in during a season of assignment. Sometimes in that season, the pain of the character development causes us to turn toward pursuing our dreams prematurely. And if we get to our dreams too fast, we find the character is not there and thus our dreams are short-lived.

If you find there is permission to pursue your dreams, then you should start exploring what that would look like while you still have provision from your current work situation. As that passion is developing inside of you that you hope someday can become your life, start small, and find a way to develop alongside of your present work. That way you have some resources to live off, and the pain of making such a sudden transition won't devastate you financially, but will do what it is intended to do: take you higher in favor and influence. I have observed people who lost the grace working at their job, but they didn't want to pursue a change because they had been comfortable in that work position for so many years and it had become very easy for them. When our salaried position is predictable and assured and the working relationships are good, we think, *Why change a good thing?* And yet, God is always inviting us into something greater. I have heard people prophesying over these same individuals about specific things to pursue, things that do require a change, but they were too scared to change their circumstances, and a transition just seemed too daunting.

Step Out of Your Comfort Zone

In one relationship of mine, I could see the change coming two years prior. I kept asking them, "Do you see that change coming? Are you listening to the prophetic words regarding stepping into new things?"

"Oh," they replied, "I don't want to do those new things. I like it right where I am at." Well after several years, their job was taken over by someone else. Now they are working a 9-5 job very different than what they are called to, and they are a bit bitter at life and their current circumstances. They aren't even going to church anymore. I could tell you countless stories of similar situations. People sometimes have such a hard time agreeing with the curve in the road that is really for their own good. God will often move us into a different way of doing things so we can grow in receiving more from Him. If you could begin making the change now while the financial provision is available, you could step into the new season with acceleration instead of the deficit of barely scraping by.

Most folks who have a hard time stepping out of the predictability of a stable job even though it is boring to them, do so because they are under the false belief they are secure in it. The truth of the matter is, it isn't even that secure. I mean, for some of my friends, their so-called "secure" job was barely bringing in what they needed. The truth is, they stay because it is familiar. But you must be willing to break out of the familiar and out of your comfort zone in order to step into a new rhythm God has prepared for you. You have to be willing to embrace a new level of trust in God, face fresh fears head on with greater grace, and pursue the resources God has put *within* you. These will become your fruitful harvest of provision. There's no other way.

The Israelites couldn't get this one worked out very easily. They wanted to be free of the tyranny of Egypt, but when they actually got free, they wanted to return to the predictable life of bondage. Freedom was just too scary, and they had to rely on God to the degree that made them exceedingly uncomfortable. God was offering them a wonderful new homeland of opportunity with favor, houses, and lands they hadn't worked for, and gardens, orchards, and vineyards of bountiful harvests they hadn't labored in. They couldn't step into it though because they feared the scary unknown and the giants terrified them. Instead, they had to die in the desert until the next generation of warriors grew up and said, "Let's take that land. . . . We can do it!" I want to encourage you to be like Caleb, who as an 85-year-old man declared, "Give me that mountain God promised!"

> *Now then, just as the LORD promised, he has kept me alive for forty-five years since the time he said this to Moses, while Israel moved about in the wilderness. So here I am today, eighty-five years old! I am still as strong today as the day Moses sent me out; I'm just as vigorous to go out to battle now as I was then. Now give me this hill country that the LORD promised me that day. You yourself heard then that the Anakites were there*

*and their cities were large and fortified, but, the
LORD helping me, I will drive them out just as he
said.*

Joshua 14:10-12

Listen to that courage from Caleb and be one that says, *No matter the mountain in front of me, I can do this! I will work hard to learn the skills to become a resource. I have what it takes to prosper in this season. I will be blessed!*

In the next chapter, I want to dig deeper into the identity you must internally possess that will sustain you as a resource. Identity is the doorway to access becoming a person of value that attracts resources.

QUESTIONS TO PONDER

1. What resources do you have? List them here.

_____

_____

_____

2. What is the first step you could take with the resources you have to begin to see them developed?

_____

_____

3. What fears are keeping you from stepping out and letting your resources start working for you?

_____

_____

4. What would your resources look like if they grew to become something much more? How could they change your life and your present financial situation?

_____

_____

Five

KNOW WHO YOU ARE

*P*overty is rooted in a lack of value, and value is rooted in the depths of identity. Knowing your identity is key to breaking poverty.

For the next several years after moving to The Mission, I learned that my identity had been rooted in my job and position. I had been a senior leader at my church for over ten years, and when I thought of stepping out of that position and moving into the unknown, my mind began to race as I wrestled internally: *Will I be valued and honored outside of my present senior leader role?* It was hard for me to imagine how I would even be taken seriously without this respectable elder position, and this really shook me.

Within a year of functioning in my new position on The Mission team, the leaders took all the staff through identity training. Each staff member received prophetic words from a couple of leadership staff and then we spent some time together processing them. We broke up into groups of three and together we identified several of the most significant words out of those prophecies, such as, "good son", "prophetic voice", "courageous", "a father to the nations", etc. These prophetic words clearly pointed to the identities God declared over us. Then each person went home and crafted those words together to form an identity statement—a declaration of our personal identity as God sees us. I found the whole process really helpful.

At the next staff meeting, we were expected to stand before everyone and declare this identity statement of who we are. But I was scared spitless! For one, the staff leadership were my heroes! These were the ones I would meet with for counsel when I pastored my church in Willits, and in my eyes, they were spiritual giants! However, what I so love about being at The Mission is that you can't be there long without becoming a giant yourself. The Mission develops giants in the faith and giants know who they are.

Declaring My Identity

The staff meeting was drawing near and I prepared myself to present my own identity statement. I had one identity within my statement though, that came out of the prophetic words I had received from the leadership and strongly felt it was very much part of who I was supposed to be. But I was afraid to include it. Even though I knew it to be true, I thought it might sound a bit arrogant: *I am a prophet.* You see, for whatever reason, that word "prophet" was taboo as I was growing up, and so for me to declare it publicly would have been considered prideful. I reasoned this out before the Lord and overcame it by realizing that this was nothing more than intimidation from the enemy to inhibit me from declaring my true identity before my peers.

That night I had a significant dream from the Lord. In my dream, a prophet friend said to me, "Keith, if you don't declare your identity as a prophet, you will lose the access to what that identity is inviting you into." It was a profound truth God was revealing to me and a common mistake we sometimes make: *Those truths which we do not declare over ourselves become as unwritten checks we don't get to cash.* When I awakened from that dream, I determined to include that portion in my identity statement.

The next day during the staff meeting, my turn came. My hands were trembling as I stood before the staff. With a shaky voice, I timidly read out my short statement:

> I am Keith Brian Ferrante . . . one who is meant for the battlefield.
>
> I am a person of great authority and influence.
>
> I am teachable and entrusted with the privilege of teaching others.
>
> I am a carrier of the presence of God and a father to worshipers.
>
> I am a prophet of fire who brings revival wherever I go . . .

I sat down quickly, still shaking and relieved to be done. But as I did, one of the staff said to me, "Keith it sounds like we are torturing you. We'd like you to stand up and say it again . . . but this time, say it like you mean it!"

So I stood back up and holding my statement firmly up with my head a bit higher, I repeated each line once again with as much courage as I could muster. It wasn't great, but it was a start! Believing those things that God says about you takes time.

Maturing in an Identity Culture

Living and maturing in a strong identity culture can cause a lot of insecurities to arise. Those who have embraced who God says they are become very confident and secure in their heavenly personas. In fact, they will thrive. The ones who aren't yet secure are easily intimidated by those who live comfortably with who they are so that they are sometimes accused of being prideful and unapproachable. But in reality, insecurity is another face of poverty that will keep you from being an influencer.

As I grew strong in my identity, I began to assault every area that lacked security. I started declaring over myself:

> Doors of favor and influence are open for me to
> walk through. I am called to sit with key leaders
> and kings, influencing the course of churches,
> cities, and nations.

Within a month of making that declaration, the Lord led me through a sort of treasure hunt in a foreign country where I met significant leaders and began to build relationships with them. The door opened as a direct result of me declaring: "I am meant to influence kings." But you can't influence kings if you believe you are a pauper. If you are intimidated by someone, you will never be able to be comfortable in their presence. This inability to feel at ease with people of status will inhibit you from being an influencer and bringing the fullness of the Kingdom into that relationship.

Accessing Your Destiny

Knowing your identity is a key to you accessing your destiny. Gideon is a wonderful example of someone transformed by identity. In Judges 6:12, an angel gives Gideon his first real sword, the weapon of an identity word:

> *When the angel of the LORD appeared to Gideon,*
> *he said, "The LORD is with you, mighty warrior."*

I love the results from this word. Gideon hadn't fought a single battle, but he was called a "mighty warrior". Our senior leader, David Crone, says:

> In the Kingdom, we are called warriors before
> we have fought a battle.

The identity given through a prophetic word, a personal word from the Lord or others, is a seed. As we agree and believe that word is working in our lives, it will become a full harvest.

Notice the first response Gideon, the "mighty warrior", has when he hears this word:

> *"Pardon me, my lord," Gideon replied, "but if*
> *the LORD is with us, why has all this happened*
> *to us? . . ."*

> Judges 6:13a

This doesn't sound like the language of a mighty warrior to me, but it reflected his reality. The word began to work, exposing the areas that disagreed with the reality of the fullness of that word manifesting in Gideon's life. I remember the first time I had an identity word spoken over me. It seemed much the same way. Through a prophetic voice, someone declared over me that I was "a man of courage". Well, I seemed far removed from courage at the time; in fact, fear and intimidation more accurately described my personality. But over the course of time, I took the word that I was a man of courage and began to war with it, brought it into my circumstances, until fear began to vanish and courage began to rise within me in agreement with who God said I was. I was beginning to manifest what it looked like to be a man of courage.

Gideon was a mighty warrior; he just didn't look it to those around him yet, including himself. Through a course of confirmations and fleeces he put out, Gideon began to grow in courage. Then he had to confront his father's idols. Why do you have to confront your family's strongholds first? Because that is where the stronghold of a wrong identity can manifest itself in your life. Before you can be a mighty warrior, you have to face your siblings, your father and mother, and others from whom you have learned identity. Notice that before David could kill Goliath, he had to face the ridicule of his brother.

> *When Eliab, David's oldest brother, heard him speaking with the men, he burned with anger at him and asked, "Why have you come down here? And with whom did you leave those few sheep in the wilderness? I know how conceited you are and how wicked your heart is; you came down only to watch the battle."*
>
> 1 Samuel 17:28

What a sorry attempt to knock David down a few notches to a lowly sheepherder. It seems that Eliab should have been more respectful to David. After all, he had seen his little brother be anointed king by the national prophet Samuel. But this humbling by family members was all a part of David's training. He took a few more hits on his identity from King Saul who ridiculed him by stating he was nothing more than a weak and unskilled child. Even Goliath mocked him.

But David knew who he was, and who his God was, and the rest is history.

Gideon had a similar experience in his journey. He was required to demolish his father's idols. But that made him very afraid, so he did it under the cover of night. Surprisingly, as the angry mob rushed to kill him the next day because he had destroyed the city idols, Gideon's dad spared his life, and from that moment on, his identity in his family was elevated.

> *But Joash replied to the hostile crowd around him, "Are you going to plead Baal's cause? Are you trying to save him? Whoever fights for him shall be put to death by morning! If Baal really is a god, he can defend himself when someone breaks down his altar." So because Gideon broke down Baal's altar, they gave him the name Jerub-Baal that day, saying, "Let Baal contend with him."*

> Judges 6:31-32

Gideon no longer was the one hiding. He was actually the one who would be defended by God and others, and he began to manifest publicly what it meant to be a mighty warrior—just as God had declared over him.

Even Jesus had to go through this identity process. During His lifetime, His own brothers did not recognize Him as God. In His hometown of Nazareth, He couldn't do many miracles because they stumbled over His lesser identity: "Joseph's son", a mere carpenter.

> *All spoke well of him and were amazed at the gracious words that came from his lips. "Isn't this Joseph's son?" they asked.*
>
> Luke 4:22

They heard His words, they knew He was anointed by God, but they couldn't get over His earthly identity as Joseph's son from the little northern town of Nazareth. Notice though, that Jesus started his ministry in his own birth town. The people said, "Can anything good come out of Nazareth?"[3] But He didn't allow their opinions and ridicule to keep him from ministering there. I pastored ten years in the town where I went to high school. There is something about learning to step into who God says you are despite those who know you as, "Little Bobby," "Rebellious Suzie," "Shy Guy," or other lesser identities intended to disqualify and inhibit you from breaking out of such a confining place. Old identities, negative pasts, and even failed histories all try to imprison you in a place of poverty, defeat, and brokenness. But God will always speak your true identity to show you how He sees you so you can break free and apprehend the victory that is your eternal destiny.

Identity Shift: From Fearful to Warrior

Let's go back a moment to see the final success of Gideon's transformation from a fearful, powerless individual to a victorious general of an army and potential leader of his nation. Gideon weeded out the army of every individual who was scared and those who wanted to go home until they were only a mere 300. He got all the way up to game day—the day he was going to confront the enemy— and what is the strategy that he announced to his 300?

> *"Watch me," he told them. "Follow my lead. When I get to the edge of the camp, do exactly as I do. When I and all who are with me blow our trumpets, then from all around the camp blow yours and shout, 'For the LORD and for Gideon.'"*
>
> Judges 7:17-18

True leadership can say with full confidence, "Watch me . . . follow my lead . . . do exactly as I do." Gideon changed from fearfully hiding out from those who might do him harm to leading an army of elite military troops—300 fearless warriors. The ultimate victory came out of a declaration that Gideon led his warriors to shout out: "A sword for the Lord and for Gideon." *What?* Hey, we would have no problem saying: *In the name of Jesus, we declare victory!* But here Gideon declared, *In the name of the Lord and Gideon we are going to see victory today.* Wow. That's a confident warrior who knows his God and knows who he is in God.

Gideon came full circle, from a small man to a mighty warrior. This is the very place where we must all come to if we want to break poverty's cycle in our lives.

Fast-track Transformation

In a previous chapter, we talked about Paul Potts, the timid singer from the UK talent show. It is fascinating to observe the transformation of the contestants as they move from the initial tryouts to where they pass each judge-hurdle and advance through each round right on to the winner's circle over a period of months. At first, they are so excited that they made it simply through the first tryouts. They scream, cry, jump around with joy, and extend their heartfelt thanks to all who helped them get to that point and on to the next level. As the show continues to air and they progress each week, you hear their language of identity and aspiration begin to change. At first, they can't believe they made it past the first tryout; some of them begin to dream of a living a different life beyond working at a fast food place. The contestants receive lots of affirmation by the judges, the crowds, and their growing number of fans. They also get critiqued; but the great ones rise up and grow up. With each critical analysis of their performance, they take it to heart and determine to improve their skills. By the end as people are cheering for them as they receive the victor's title, they exude confidence and are much more secure in their gift. And with the big win, they even enjoy a bit more financial security.

That is the transformation of someone who's moved out of poverty, self-doubt, and lack. The journey from the mindset of "I'm nothing but a worm," to someone who realizes, "I am valuable and have something significant to offer this world," is the transformation God wants each of us to pass through.

In the next chapter, I want to build on the identity foundation by discussing how to be protected from selling yourself as you release your gift.

QUESTIONS TO PONDER

1. What identity do you need to declare aloud to start you on your journey towards a greater destiny?

_____

_____

2. What would your identity statement look like if you were speaking about yourself the way God speaks about you? Write down at least 3 key points.

_____

_____

_____

3. In what areas in your life do you feel insignificant? Where do you cut yourself down or see yourself as less than God sees you? (For example, do you devalue your own body? Your looks, personality, lack of skills, etc.?) After you identify them, write down the opposite and positive characteristic of each negative one and consider the implications if you were to walk in your heavenly identity.

_____

_____

_____

4. Using our example of Gideon, in what areas of your identity (family idols) have not been healthy because, like Gideon, you learned a wrong belief system from your upbringing? Take time to write out incorrect family beliefs that are false that you need to change because they are contrary to what God says about you and are contrary to your destiny.

_____

_____

_____

5. Take some time to process what God has said about you by writing out descriptive words that point to your destiny—the person God sees. Then write an identity statement that declares who you really are in His eyes that you would be willing to declare in front of people. Begin each statement with "I am . . ."

_____

_____

_____

_____

_____

_____

_____

Six

NOT FOR HIRE

As I progressed toward gaining more security in my identity, I also had to pursue a healthier and more productive way to use my gifts. I had been learning that people all around the world love to hear the word of the Lord through the prophetic. I have a strong gift of prophecy and have learned to tap into the prophetic to open up heavenly atmospheres through music, prophesying, and preaching. In my journey of stepping out of salary-based finances to resource-based finances, I took every meeting I was offered just to make ends meet. Trying to make it financially and learning this new rhythm was difficult. In reality, there was no rhythm . . . only survival mode as the bills mounted.

Toward the end of those 2 years, I was traveling full time in the U.S. and abroad, taking every invitation I received from my mentors and those that came from relational connections, both old and new. It was an exciting, fast-paced and often exhausting season, but I was learning valuable lessons along the way. I was also learning how to properly manage myself among key leaders, what to do and not do in certain situations. I was discovering how to stay physically healthy with a demanding schedule of 20 to 30 meetings over a 10-day trip, often on foreign soil.

There came a point where several overseas meetings were canceled and had to be rescheduled for the following year for a variety of reasons. At first, I was wondering what it all meant, but quickly I had a sense that the Lord wanted me to have a break at home and focus on specific areas of my life. I began to reflect over the previous couple years of accelerated ministry.

A Grief in My Soul

As wonderful as it was to meet new people, travel overseas to new nations, learn a new life rhythm, etc., I began to examine a very specific anguish in my soul that emerged from time to time in a few regions I had traveled. It was clear that I needed to make a proper adjustment. I had observed that, at times, I had been invited solely for my prophetic gift and the ability I carried to listen to the Spirit and break open the heavens. While I appreciated their desire for spiritual breakthrough, and I certainly was most willing to see it through, I often felt used and completely spent at the end of those meetings. There was little to no genuine pursuit of relationship . . . it was all about the output of my prophetic gifts. Without a doubt this was no one's intention to make me feel used, but these incidents revealed a deeper issue in my own heart that needed to be addressed.

Discovering My Value

As I pondered the sting of feeling used because of my gifts, I had to learn how to understand and accept that I am valuable—with or without the activation of my gifts. When I first started as an itinerant minister, I sort of felt like those contestants presenting themselves at their first talent tryout. Like them I would wonder to myself: *Do I have what it takes? Will people like me? Do I have something to offer that is valuable?* As time went on, I began to realize that I did indeed have what it takes. But I also learned that in order to function at my best as a prophetic voice I would have to communicate that I wasn't a prophesying machine, available for each and every person in attendance. My underlying fear was if I did share what I needed, they wouldn't invite me back. Yet at the same time, the demands on my gift were simply unworkable—to prophesy whenever and wherever . . . turned on at will, so to speak.

Growing up I was taught a very strict ministry work ethic, and I am a very hard worker. But in this context, it didn't feel like I just needed to buck up and get in there and work harder. The fact is, many times I spent days prophesying over hundreds of people, preaching many times a week, going from one place to the next with very little relational engagement in between. At first, it was all a great adventure, but soon I began to experience its effects—feeling drained physically, mentally, and spiritually—and I was convinced that I was not meant to function in this way, nor was it how God intended me to work with my gift.

I soon discovered my main mandate as a prophetic voice wasn't to be the one doing all the prophesying and the prophetic ministry, but to be the one *training others* to do the work of the ministry. Learning to value yourself means you have to get a revelation of what works best for you and what doesn't, and be courageous enough to communicate what you need.

I had a prophetic friend that was seasoned in the prophetic ministry and he helped bring some revelation on this change in my season. "Keith," he said, "you have learned that you can prophesy whenever you need to, but the season has changed. You have to see yourself as a king. Kings have an authority and call people to them when they have a word to give them. You need to move from being everyone's easy word to giving the word of the Lord that will affect key leaders and influencers that God has called you to influence."

That timely word resonated with my spirit and I knew I was definitely moving into that season.

Identity and Boundaries

While I agree everyone needs a prophetic word, a prophet's primary job isn't to do that. There are exceptions, of course, but a prophet's main job is to release vision for people to see what the Spirit is saying so each one can learn to access God for himself.

Although I had implemented this new course of action for my prophetic ministry, it didn't come easily. It was hard to refuse repeated pressured requests for personal prophetic ministry, but I did. I began to firmly tell people no, and I think I may have hurt some feelings along the way with the strength of my refusal. But as I was transitioning into this new place, I just didn't feel like giving a prophetic word, and often my response was not very nice. I remember even jokingly responding to someone with, "If you want me to give you a word, where is the fee for my services?!!" That's just how I felt . . . like I was for hire. I had functioned so long as the one who would give a prophetic word on cue that it was difficult for people to adjust to the new not-for-hire Keith. When you have walked in a certain way for a long while, but then you transform into a new identity, it takes time for everyone to adjust to the new you. Every increase in identity brings a sense of loss to those around you, and people must choose for themselves if they want to embrace the new you, reject the new you, or try to draw you back into the person you used to be. Meanwhile, you must maintain your God-given identity!

Everywhere I went I had to share the different season I had entered. I remember dreading going to several Asian nations because I had previously demonstrated that I was the prophetic joyful carrier of revival who prophesied over everyone. They loved what I carried because I brought prophetic signs and wonders and breakthrough as I ministered. A strange thing began to happen to me, however, as I made this metamorphosis: *the prophetic literally lifted from me!* I couldn't access it at all. It just wasn't there. Part of the reason was God, but the other part was my soul grieved when I felt people were *expecting* me to give them a word on cue—as if I could be bought. But I pressed through and courageously found a way to communicate my boundaries, even though it was awkward at first. Not everyone was happy about this transition, mind you. They wanted the old Keith to perform.

This lesson came to a head when I was in a nation where people were overly generous with me financially with lavish provisions, accommodations, and expensive gifts, but with it came the implied expectation for a personal prophetic word. But I committed to being obedient to how God was leading me even though I realized that I may disappoint and lose these key connections and not be invited back to their nation. On that trip, I absolutely received no personal prophetic words for any of them. The only function of my prophetic gift was within the corporate setting of teaching or prophesying over a church.

One night, a group of leaders and others met with me, and it was a real test of my resolve to not cave in to the prophet-for-hire pressure. These were key and very influential people in this particular nation who had been particularly generous to me. But I had nothing to give them in return except my friendship . . . the prophetic had been switched off. It quickly became very awkward as I realized their true intentions: They expected I would spend the entire evening prophesying over each one of them.

I knew I had to address this uncomfortable situation, so I said to them, "Guys, do you know how to prophesy? How many of you hear God?" I spent the next several minutes talking with them about developing a prophetic culture instead of waiting each year for a prophetic word from the guest prophet. Now they weren't totally to blame. I had been a part of creating this expectation because of how I had previously operated in my gifts. But unfortunately, these leaders were not as receptive to my idea of being trained in the prophetic as I had hoped.

Then the host family where I was staying invited some leaders over to their beautiful home for the very same reason, fully expecting me to prophesy over each one of them. But I had already informed them that I didn't have anything prophetic to give, so it was another awkward evening.

I continued to minister in this nation while wrestling through my position of not-for-hire, but it was clear to see from the leaders' responses that I was not meeting their expectations of personal prophecy. They didn't understand my new position nor did they appreciate it.

I was doing one final meeting in this nation, and at the end of the service, the pastor asked if I would be a part of the ministry team when I finished preaching. "Sure!" I answered. I really love to minister to people in the right context, especially in a corporate setting. As the ministry time started, everyone rushed up to have me pray for them. It didn't seem to matter who else was up at the altar. I was the only one they wanted to pray over them. I prayed for one after another, but the line of those waiting for prayer ministry seemed endless so that I finally announced, "I need to use the restroom!"—my excuse to take a break. But passing to and from the restroom, people were pulling me aside and pressing me for prophetic words and personal prayer. I was at the point of distress when I pleaded with the pastor, "Please . . . I need a quiet room in the back where I can rest!" It was all just too much for me.

I loved this nation so much and was really blessed to be a part of what God was doing there. But by this time, I was pretty sure I would not be invited back, and it pained me as I thought about it. Yet at the same time, I knew the clear boundaries God had firmly established for me was because He valued me, He valued my gifts, and He desired them to be most productive. His boundaries for me guaranteed a healthy protection from such intolerable ministry conditions.

A Heavenly Perspective

As I rested in the back room of the church following such an evening of intense prayer ministry, the Lord began to speak to me about the poverty spirit. He said, "Keith, it doesn't matter how many times you prophesy or lay hands on those with a poverty spirit, it will never be enough. What they need is a revelation of My son, Jesus." He then led me to the passage in Philippians:

> *I am not saying this because I am in need, for I have learned to be content whatever the circumstances. I know what it is to be in need, and I know what it is to have plenty. I have*

learned the secret of being content in any and every situation, whether well fed or hungry, whether living in plenty or in want. I can do all this through him who gives me strength.

4:11-13

The Lord continued: "Keith, people need to get a revelation that they already have enough. So many people think if only I can get one more word, one more prayer, a little more of His love, then I will know that everything is going to be okay; then I will be able to make it." This is a poverty spirit or an orphan spirit in full operation. Orphans have a hole in the bottom of their love bucket, and as much as you pour into them, it is *never* enough. And it doesn't matter if you have lots of money or no money at all, you can still possess a poverty spirit. At times, wealthy people can use their riches to try to buy affection, encouragement, or whatever they need just to boost their own worth. Others will try to show how needy they are in hopes that someone will give them a handout of pity by feeling sorry for them. An orphan spirit or a poverty mentality craves pity and is endlessly needy. But soliciting pity is never the right way to get a need met. The answer to breaking a poverty-orphan spirit is found in Galatians:

And because you are sons, God sent forth the Spirit of His Son into your hearts, crying out, "Abba, Father!" Therefore you are no longer a slave but a son, and if a son, then an heir of God through Christ.

4:6-7, NKJV

Adoption by our Father in Heaven breaks that spirit for good.

I love that we are no longer without an inheritance, because we are the King's sons and daughters. The Spirit of God is crying out within us, "Daddy, Daddy!" I spent years seeking to get filled up by well-known spiritual fathers and mothers. They poured into me many words of encouragement and affirmation, and yet, I still responded out of an orphan spirit. One day I received a transforming revelation that the Father's answer to our need for love was to send Jesus. Jesus is inside of me crying out, "Daddy, Daddy!" When I received that revelation, somewhere from deep within my own spirit I literally cried out, "Daddy, Daddy!" and knew that Jesus was crying out. I felt the shift. I didn't have a question in my heart any longer that asked, *Am I really loved? Do I have enough? Do I need another prayer, another talk, another hug, another prophecy?* I knew I had enough because I had Jesus inside of me.

Jesus is the Answer

I know it sounds so simple, but Jesus really is the answer to every problem that this world has. He is the answer for the orphan. He is the answer to poverty. The revelation Paul shared about having enough whether he had little or much began to make sense. He knew that Jesus inside of him never lacked because Jesus never had a struggle with needing more. If He had only five loaves of bread and two small fish but thousands to feed, He knew the key was in the giving thanks to God.

> *Then some boats from Tiberias landed near the place where the people had eaten the bread after the Lord had given thanks.*
>
> John 6:23

You see, in Jesus, if you give away a piece of pie in the Kingdom, you get two pieces of pie in return, because there is no lack. The little you have is always multiplied to produce more. That is why whether you have little or much, it is *always* enough . . . even more than enough!

Endless Supply

One time I noticed we were getting low on laundry detergent, and so I told my wife, "Heather, we need to get some detergent." But for whatever reason, we didn't purchase it. But the nearly empty container of detergent continued to pour out into the measuring cup for many more loads of laundry, even for several weeks! We could see the laundry soup was down to the bottom, yet it continued to pour. The Lord was blowing my mind through that miracle showing me that in the Kingdom, there is a never-ending supply. It's bottomless! *Yes!* There is *always* enough. In the glory, there is every provision for all that is needed.

> *And my God will meet all your needs according to the riches of his glory in Christ Jesus.*
>
> Philippians 4:19

The Greek word translated "needs"[4] refers to employment, jobs, business, needs and wants. In Christ, all our jobs, employment, needs and wants are provided for in His glory.

Heaven's Measure

There are rooms in Heaven full of more than enough. That is why Jesus says:

> *My Father's house has many rooms; if that were*

*not so, would I have told you that I am going
there to prepare a place for you?*

John 14:2

I used to think those rooms meant that when we die and go
to Heaven, we will finally be able to enjoy mansion-sized rooms
of our own. What good is a mansion going to be for us when we
are in glory? Ephesians 2:6 says:

*And God raised us up with Christ and seated us
with him in the heavenly realms in Christ Jesus.*

These rooms are not for some distant future when we die.
We are seated in heavenly places *right now*. We get to learn how
to explore those heavenly rooms that are meant for us. There
are rooms of provision for whatever we need—body parts for
healing, business strategies, answers to governmental issues,
and so much more.

I have actually entered some of the heavenly rooms. I
remember praying the theophany of Revelation chapter one
where Jesus is walking amongst the seven golden lampstands.
As I was meditating on that passage I began to get ideas for
some business strategies I really needed. My mind sparked, and
I realized, *Oh my! I am in my Spirit standing right amongst the
golden lampstands, so why wouldn't there be financial answers
in the midst of the glory of Heaven's atmosphere?* "On earth as it
is in Heaven" is our cry. There is no poverty or lack in Heaven;
Heaven is within us through Christ.

*"Nor will they say, 'See here!' or 'See there!' For
indeed, the kingdom of God is within you."*

Luke 17:21, NKJV

We have to learn to access and manifest the measure of Heaven where we are seated and which is seated in us.

We are no longer poor orphans. We have a rich Daddy, and everything He has is ours.

"My son," the father said, "you are always with me, and everything I have is yours."

Luke 15:31

In Christ, we have our inheritance, and everything we need is readily available. We get to go on an adventure to find out how to access all the wonderful rooms He has prepared for us.

Costly Gifts from Dad

All of these experiences I've shared here have been part of God's process to break off poverty in my life by pointing to how He values me. Remember, poverty is a lack of understanding your own value. If you don't understand your value, you won't be able to declare your value, walk as a valued one, and see the blessings given to you as a valued one. Whenever subjects come before their kings, they bring gifts. Not because kings need them, but to show their honor and appreciation for them. We are Dad's kids. He is the King of kings and we are one of the kings over whom He reigns as King. We ought to be able to receive His gifts with no expectation of reciprocating. I was soon to have a vivid example of that.

I received two very costly gifts from individuals that I met only briefly: a Harley Davidson Sportster motorcycle and a Steinway grand piano. Each gift was a kiss from Heaven and it really touched my heart so deeply. With each of these gifts,

I sensed the Father saying, "Son, I love to give you things that you didn't work for just to show you that you are Mine. Not everything comes from your own effort, and sometimes I give good gifts just because I love you and want to lavish blessings on you."

I'm not just hired help; I am his much-loved son. Dad's generosity is a continual reminder of how much He values us.

In the next chapter, I want to explore in greater depth how your view of God determines what is available to you.

QUESTIONS TO PONDER

1. Is there a situation in your life (at work, in your relationships, in ministry or church) where you have felt like a "prophet-for-hire" where you felt used? Spend some time to ask God for a pathway out of that unhealthy place.

2. Are there boundaries you need to review and/or establish that will protect you and your gifts?

3. In what ways has the poverty and/or orphan spirit manifested in your life?

_____

_____

4. List the ways in which God has shown you recently how much He values you.

_____

_____

5. Consider your inheritance in Christ and the riches of the Kingdom available to you. What is the upgrade God is inviting you into?

_____

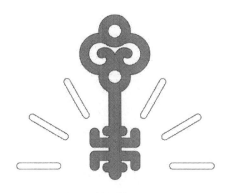

$\mathcal{S}even$

GOD IS A RICH KING

$\mathcal{Y}$our view of Jesus determines everything for you. Let me explain. I grew up with the mindset that serving Jesus meant being poor. It was almost like, the poorer you are, the more spiritual you are. This belief says, *We can't take anything with us so we better get to laying up treasure in Heaven instead of enjoying it down here.* As a preacher's kid I experienced this firsthand. It seemed that most pastors I knew, including my parents and grandparents, didn't have much. It even reflected in the housing provided for the pastor by the church. When my wife and I began pastoring, we lived in a church parsonage for seven years with a leaky roof and mold on the walls. Consequently, my wife suffered repeated health issues because of it. Living in these kind of impoverished conditions was all too common for those in the pastorate, and sadly, they were to be expected.

But it especially grieved me to see my parents and friends in pastoral ministry living such meager lives, many of them just barely getting by. Most of the pastors I knew were weighed down with the tremendous burden of financial concerns. Added to their own personal concerns, they also carried the load of the church's finances, and sometimes had to even cover ministry expenses out of their own pockets, which the church body should have done.

My heart cried out in such times, "God! There must be a different way! Help us get a true revelation of who You are." I knew we needed a greater revelation of Jesus in order to see a greater manifestation of Heaven in our lives and circumstances. As Paul says:

> *I keep asking that the God of our Lord Jesus Christ, the glorious Father, may give you the Spirit of wisdom and revelation, so that you may know him better.*
>
> Ephesians 1:17

This was my heart's cry in that season—to know Him better!

A Poor-King View

One day, Jesus spoke with me and said, "Keith, I have wanted to bless you . . . really I have! But you only see Me as a *poor* King, and your perspective inhibits Me blessing you in the extravagance of my true nature."

Ouch! That stung! But His words broke through.

Sometimes we think the answer to a breakthrough would be a greater effort on our part, when in reality, the start to receiving the answer is a greater revelation of God. My view of God as a poor King was attracting poverty to my life because that is exactly how I viewed God. I was living it because that is what I expected! I saw spirituality as how much material or earthly possessions you could *give up* for Him; I felt shame owning anything of substance or earthly value. It seemed extravagant to me and not pleasing to God.

I remember how guilty I felt when we bought our first house. I was tormented by thoughts of how others might perceive it: *People in my church may wonder if I am squandering their money . . . They'll think the money they give in the offering is for my own personal comfort, or something . . .* I had some maturing to do.

This poverty view was causing me to suffer in the most foundational of God's provisions for me—housing. My view of Jesus was of that poor little babe born in a lowly manger with no real bed upon which to lay his poor little head. I interpreted the Scriptures of Jesus asking His disciples to give up *everything* to follow Him (I believed that meant He was requiring pretty much everything you own) to where you're basically living like a homeless disciple wandering the earth looking for a handout. On the other hand, I regularly quoted the Scripture that states God owns the cattle on a thousand hills;[5] I knew everything belonged to Father God! But my skewed view of 'poor Jesus' was harming my ability to access the wealth of Heaven. It is a double-minded belief: God is rich, but Jesus is poor. Those inconsistent views of God neutralized what was meant to be powerful and potent, kind of like when you combine fire and ice. What do you get? Just some lukewarm water.

The Little-to-Nothing Lens

My inaccurate view of God sent me on a study through the Scriptures where a whole new understanding emerged. Here I want to add a word of caution. It's amazing how you can support the perspective you already have in Scripture when you look for it. Anyone who has a strong belief system in a specific area will see from *that* viewpoint and finding a verse will only reinforce what they already believe. Even cults become so convinced about what they believe because they see through the lens they put on. So if your lens views Jesus as poor, then everything you see in Scripture will validate it. You will end up finding all the verses that highlight impoverished conditions: the poor widow who gave her last two cents, those who were down to a single loaf of bread, the needy who begged pitifully for help, and Jesus born in a dirty animal stable with only a straw manger for a bed. Other Scriptures prove that unless you give it all up, you can't be a disciple, or how "the Son of Man has no place to lay his head"[6] (inferring a pitiful, homeless state). Scriptures like these become reinforcements to a stronghold of a poverty mindset with a convincing paradigm that says, *As Jesus lived on earth with little to nothing, so should I.*

But everything in the Bible isn't meant to be the example of how we should live, nor are we supposed to follow every biblical character presented. For instance, some people see Job's physical afflictions and Paul's "thorn in the flesh" as proof that Jesus doesn't heal everyone and that, we, too, should expect infirmities. This belief system suggests, Jesus *can* certainly heal, but He doesn't always heal, nor does He heal everyone. But let's remember that Jesus is the model, not Paul, not Job, not Peter, or any of the other apostles or prophets or biblical characters. We can certainly learn from those who lived in the biblical period, and we should draw courage by their bravery and journey to faith despite the obstacles.

Heaven's Unfathomable Abundance Lens

It became very clear to me that I needed the lens of the Holy Spirit to see the glorified Jesus in the Scriptures.

When we look at who Jesus is, it only points us to the unfathomable abundance that is in God. Our focus is redirected from a poverty mindset to the endless riches readily available for all we could ever need. Have you ever considered the fact that although Jesus was born in a dirty stable with the animals, very wealthy kings came to that humble place with extravagant and costly gifts of gold, frankincense, and myrrh? Studies estimate that the amount of those gifts to be about one million U.S. dollars, according to today's value. These weren't just nomads riding on camels across the desert with some trinkets; they were highly influential and wealthy rulers. Their status and prestige easily afforded them an audience before King Herod.[7] When Herod learned they were in the region of his jurisdiction around Jerusalem, he secretly called for them and inquired about their mission. They had come from countries very far away from Israel to bring the newborn costly gifts fit for a King. Without a doubt, those gifts sustained Jesus and his family for the period of time they had to flee Bethlehem and hide out in Egypt, and perhaps even aided their repatriation following Herod's death.

Jesus understands the financial needs we have to live life and He patterned the proper relationship with money and wealth. Joseph, Jesus' earthly dad, was a carpenter and businessman, and Jesus worked alongside of him in the family business prior to his own ministry at the age of 30. When Jesus selected His disciples with His heavenly Father's help, many of these were businessmen as well: a doctor, a tax collector, seven fishermen who had lucrative businesses in the fishing industry, etc. For instance, the two "sons of Zebedee" were business owners with their father who hired other men to work for them. Without a doubt these businesses continued to prosper, even as the disciples were occupied with their itinerant work and one-on-one training alongside of Jesus.

The financing of Jesus' itinerant ministry came from some of the women who followed him, including a prominent supporter who was Herod's household manager.

> *Mary (called Magdalene) from whom seven demons had come out; Joanna the wife of Chuza, the manager of Herod's household; Susanna; and many others. These women were helping to support them out of their own means.*
>
> Luke 8:2b, 3

The flow of funds into Jesus' ministry actually required a treasurer, and we know that Judas was the appointed one for this job.

Jesus often spoke about possessions, money, and wealth in an attempt to prioritize its hold on our heart and mind as well as to highlight Kingdom values. Sometimes we can read a Scripture and make an assumption, like this one:

> *Do not take a purse or bag or sandals . . .*
>
> Luke 10:4a

From this we may conclude that Jesus meant we are not to possess anything at all. But later on, He gives further instruction to His followers on this subject:

> *Then Jesus asked them, "When I sent you without purse, bag or sandals, did you lack anything?"*

"Nothing," they answered.

He said to them, "But now if you have a purse, take it, and also a bag; and if you don't have a sword, sell your cloak and buy one."

Luke 22:35-36

Some people camp out with such Scriptures in an attempt to validate their own lack and impoverished state of mind. The point that Jesus is making in these differing circumstances is that in one season, you aren't supposed to be weighed down with anything extra because you have a specific and urgent mission; instead you're to trust God's daily provision for all you need in order to stay focused on the task at hand. But in the other season, you are instructed to receive and enjoy everything He gives you. In fact, if you don't have it, find a way to purchase it.

So the question is, which season are you in? Are you putting your trust in what you are able to make or in God's greater provision? It is important that we settle forever our motivation and who is our provider. God entrusts some people with financial fortunes and lavish housing provisions, while to others He gives a more modest but sufficient measure. The measure and amount is irrelevant as we choose to live with an abundant mindset. It's vitally important that we look to our heavenly Father as our primary source and steward His abundant provision conscientiously and with gratitude.

In Whom Do You Trust?

In the passage about the rich young ruler we often misunderstand its primary message. I used to think: *God must want me to give up everything and live as a pauper because that's what He asked of the rich young ruler.* No, he was simply probing to see if the rich young ruler lived for riches primarily or if his riches served him.

When Jesus heard this, he said to him, "You still lack one thing. Sell everything you have and give to the poor, and you will have treasure in heaven. Then come, follow me."

When he heard this, he became very sad, because he was very wealthy. Jesus looked at him and said, "How hard it is for the rich to enter the kingdom of God! Indeed, it is easier for a camel to go through the eye of a needle than for someone who is rich to enter the kingdom of God."

Those who heard this asked, "Who then can be saved?"

Jesus replied, "What is impossible with man is possible with God."

Peter said to him, "We have left all we had to follow you!"

"Truly I tell you," Jesus said to them, "no one who has left home or wife or brothers or sisters or parents or children for the sake of the kingdom of God will fail to receive many times as much in this age, and in the age to come eternal life."

Luke 18:22-30

I never caught the last part until years after I had read that passage so many times. It says that those who give up homes for His sake will receive "many times as much in this age." In several of the other gospels, this passage says we will receive a hundredfold. That is a wonderful promise! Jesus wasn't instructing those of us who follow Him to live at poverty level. He needed to determine that this young man's wealth didn't *own* him. In this example Jesus is directing our motivation and focus to a higher realm instead of working for more and more money. That's where our real investment security lies. If the young rich man would have given up the whole lot to serve Him, Jesus told His disciples, he would have received the promise from Heaven of so much more in return—a hundredfold increase, in fact. That is better than any financial investment plan ever devised. All Jesus was trying to do in this instance was settle an issue of trust with this young man. The question is always: **In whom do you trust?** Is it God? Once you know the answer to that question, God's role as sole provider in your life is restored to its rightful place. Our priority, then, is not to work for riches, but to serve Him first so that the return to us will be much more than we could ever imagine.

God's Nature Redeems and Restores

I shared in my book, *There Must Be More*, about my incredible journey of the purchase and sale of my first house. As I said before, we had to foreclose our home to move to a different location because we were pursuing the greater dream in our destiny. Four years later, however, we were finally able to purchase a second home in Vacaville. It is wonderful to see that God always remembers sacrifice, and when He sees a sacrificial offering from the heart, He will repay. In one season we gave up all, and in the next season, we gained many generous gifts from our Father in return. Each season has a different lesson, but as we pass through them, God teaches us different aspects of His nature. The lesson I learned? You just cannot out-give God.

Consider the story of Job, one of the wealthiest and wisest men alive at that time.

> *And he owned seven thousand sheep, three thousand camels, five hundred yoke of oxen and five hundred donkeys, and had a large number of servants. He was the greatest man among all the people of the East.*
>
> 1:3

A stronghold of a poverty mindset is fueled with fearful and anxious thoughts. We can read the story of Job and worry ourselves sick with thoughts like: *A disaster could strike . . . my house could all go up in flames! I could lose everything! Something terrible could happen to my children . . .* But why wouldn't we, instead, want to keep our mind fixed on the latter part of Job's life?

> *After Job had prayed for his friends, the LORD restored his fortunes and gave him twice as much as he had before. All his brothers and sisters and everyone who had known him before came and ate with him in his house. They comforted and consoled him over all the trouble the LORD had brought on him, and each one gave him a piece of silver and a gold ring. The LORD blessed the latter part of Job's life more than the former part. He had fourteen thousand sheep, six thousand camels, a thousand yoke of oxen and a thousand*

donkeys. And he also had seven sons and three daughters.

42:10-13

God restored Job to be twice as prosperous as he was at first, his daughters were the most beautiful in all the land, and all his children received rich inheritances.

Nowhere in all the land were there found women as beautiful as Job's daughters, and their father granted them an inheritance along with their brothers.

Job 42:15

What a wonderful picture of redemption. But then, Job had a proper view of His Redeemer, and was a wealthy person who lost it all but received a double-portion return. Proverbs speaks about the godly blessed with wealth:

A good person leaves an inheritance for their children's children, but a sinner's wealth is stored up for the righteous.

13:22

Those with this mindset have an understanding that possessions, money, and favor will always end up back in their court. Their children and their children's children will be blessed because of it. I've heard it said that if you take away all the money in the world and distribute it evenly, in a short while, the rich will be rich again, and the poor will be poor again. Money is not given to people of stature; rather, it comes to those who are trained in wise financial and economic management principles, and who conduct their business affairs accordingly. Clearly Job held a high value on integrity and managed his household and business by a godly code of ethics attracting God's double-portion blessing.

As we continue to search through Scripture for evidence of poverty versus wealth, we find many characters besides Job were also listed among the wealthiest and most influential of their time. King Solomon was in a category all his own. It is said that the temple he built for God took billions of dollars to construct. His father, King David, had saved up most of the money in his lifetime, acquired from the years of battle and conquest and designated specifically for the construction of the temple.

Another example is Joseph, the son of Jacob, who became second in command over all of Egypt. He too was one of the wealthiest and most influential men of his time. He had such a wealthy mindset that he acquired enough food during a severe famine to save the entire region through his wisdom. Who knows what would have happened if Joseph had given in to a poverty mindset that believed, *This can never be done. It's just impossible. There's no way we can amass enough food to feed all of Egypt and the surrounding nations as well. It'll never work.* But God made sure Joseph kept his sights upon Him—a higher realm of unimaginable abundance and riches and wisdom—where he could see endless possibilities because He knew His God.

A Wealthy and Prosperous Mindset

Poverty really is a mindset that creates a reality that is less than what God intends us to have. Our view of God determines how much of what is already His we get to enjoy. Let's review the passage that Jesus shares about the prodigal "sons". I say "sons" because both of the brothers had really strayed from godliness and righteousness. One left home and squandered his inheritance, while the elder son drifted away in his heart.

> *The older brother became angry and refused to go in. So his father went out and pleaded with him. But he answered his father, "Look! All these years I've been slaving for you and never disobeyed your orders. Yet you never gave me even a young goat so I could celebrate with my friends. But when this son of yours who has squandered your property with prostitutes comes home, you kill the fattened calf for him!"*
>
> *"My son," the father said, "you are always with me, and everything I have is yours."*
>
> Luke 15:28-31

Here the older brother stayed home all those years while his younger brother wasted his resources in a foreign land. Yet the elder son had not fully possessed the wealth his father made available to him. He hadn't even tasted of the riches with which his father would have loved him to enjoy. So to his complaints he answered, "Son, you are living so below what I have given you, but all I have is yours!" What a revelation. Doesn't this sound like so many other Scriptures? Look at what Paul says in the following verses about what we have in Christ:

> *Whether Paul or Apollos or Cephas or the world or life or death or the present or the future—**all are yours, and you are of Christ, and Christ is of God.***
>
> 1 Corinthians 3:22-23, emphasis added

> *For you know the grace of our Lord Jesus Christ, that though he was rich, yet for your sake he became poor, so that you* **through his poverty might become rich.**
>
> 2 Corinthians 8:9, emphasis added

The word "rich"[8] in the Greek means, "increased with goods; rich; wealthy." I want to propose to you that Jesus did become poor compared to His residence in Heaven, but He never lived in *lack* that resembled poverty while He was here on earth. He had everything He needed at all times. If He needed anything more, He simply gave thanks to His Father who would then multiply what He already had. Anything less than this view, is an accusation against God's plentiful provision readily available to us.

God's Prosperous Nature Provides Wealth

Because we don't understand it and are afraid of appearing less than spiritual, we often interpret "wealth" as something spiritual. For example, we talk about joy, peace, love, and salvation as all we could ever need. And yet Jesus promised us in both Covenants bountiful riches of earthly provision in lands, food, clothes, etc. He just instructs us not to make it our priority.

> *But seek first his kingdom and his righteousness, and all these things will be given to you as well.*
>
> Matthew 6:33

All the things we need have been provided. Jesus Himself became poor in order that in Him, we can enjoy life to its fullest—wealth as He intends for the godly. The main focus of our lives is always His presence, of course. But He always generously provides what we need to live, eat, be clothed and satisfied with life.

> *When you have eaten and are satisfied, praise the Lord your God for the good land he has given you.*
>
> Deuteronomy 8:10

Notice "land" is included. God knows we need "land" upon which to build homes, plant gardens, and have a place to raise our children. He also is the one who generously provides what we need to invest what He gives us to live well. He actually gives us the ability to make wealth:

> *But remember the LORD your God, for it is He who gives you the ability to produce wealth . . .*
>
> v 18

He is so good that serving Him isn't about one or the other—either God and His service or an abundance of earthly goods. The main thing is that the "goodies" are a blessing from God, and He is the source of it all.

> *Praise the LORD, my soul, and forget not all his benefits—who forgives all your sins and heals all your diseases, who redeems your life from the pit and crowns you with love and compassion, who satisfies your desires with good things so that your youth is renewed like the eagle's.*
>
> Psalm 103:2-5

He does not supply love and compassion alone, but also satisfies all our desires with "good things" as well. We can have an expectation of those things! The blessings of His love, compassion, healing, are all so good and fantastic. In addition to these, we also get to enjoy so many other benefits as His sons and daughters:

> *Moreover, when God gives someone wealth and possessions, and the ability to enjoy them, to accept their lot and be happy in his toil—this is a gift of God. They seldom reflect on the days of their life, because God keeps them occupied with gladness of heart.*
>
> Ecclesiastes 5:19-20

Wealth and possessions are the generous extras of God's prosperous nature He loves to share with us, because as a good Father, it gives Him great pleasure to gift His children with such good things. He knows it brings us joy, and that delights His heart.

In this chapter, I hope to have encouraged you to continue discovering the greater revelation of who Jesus really is so that your thinking makes the way for the Father's intended rich blessings and generous provisions over your life.

In the next chapter, I want to explore how generosity opens the way for blessing to flow to us and through us.

QUESTIONS TO PONDER

1. Do you have a poverty mindset that is supported by specific Scriptures that back up your viewpoint? With the help of the Holy Spirit, what is an upgraded way to see those Scriptures from a higher heavenly perspective?

_____

_____

2. Give thought to how you viewed finances growing up. Did you come from a poor family, a generous family, a wealthy family, or a stingy family? What did that do to your value system about money?

_____

_____

3. As you consider the extravagant wealth of Heaven, in what areas could you use a shift from a poverty mindset in regards to receiving the generous blessings of the Lord?

_____

_____

Eight

GENUINE GENEROSITY

rowing up in the church, I gained an unhealthy view of generosity that caused me not to want to give. As a preacher's kid living in a parsonage, and then later as a pastor living in a parsonage next door to the church, there was an expectation that we, as representatives of the church, were the designated ones to demonstrate generosity to those in need. Now, I have no problem to help those who truly are in need. But what most people didn't know is that transients would show up all hours of the day or night to our parsonage with an expectation of financial assistance. More often than not, I was unwilling to give money to able-bodied individuals. Some were clearly going from church to church expecting pastors to take care of their physical needs. I was finding it more and more difficult to keep my heart in the right place when I was already financially strapped just trying to meet my own pressing needs.

Joyful Giver

As the pastor, I felt the expectation to give way beyond my means, but it got to the place where there was no joy in it. I was simply giving out of obligation. But the Scripture is clear how we are to give:

> *Each of you should give what you have decided in your heart to give, not reluctantly or under compulsion, for God loves a cheerful giver.*
>
> 2 Corinthians 9:7

I was definitely not a cheerful giver, and on this issue, I knew my heart was not in a good place. But God was patient with me in undoing what had developed within me. I had become a reluctant giver, void of heart-felt generosity. Genuine generosity spills out of us and isn't coerced or compelled. A good example of this is how the Corinthian Church demonstrated generosity from their hearts, even in their most extreme trial:

> *In the midst of a very severe trial, their overflowing joy and their extreme poverty welled up in rich generosity. For I testify that they gave as much as they were able, and even beyond their ability. Entirely on their own, they urgently pleaded with us for the privilege of sharing in this service to the Lord's people. And they exceeded our expectations: They gave themselves first of all to the Lord, and then by the will of God also to us.*
>
> 2 Corinthians 8:2-5

Though the Corinthians were financially poor, they did not manifest poverty in their giving. In fact, they *pleaded* with Paul for the opportunity to find a way to release "rich generosity" despite their monetary lack. They desired it and found a way to bless God and His people anyway. Their motives to give were not to impress others, but to be generous to the Lord. As it says in Proverbs:

> *Whoever is kind to the poor lends to the LORD,*
> *and he will reward them for what they have done.*
>
> 19:17

What they lacked in monetary means, they expressed in rich generosity out of what they did possess. Because they were lending to the Lord, they were assured He would certainly repay them abundantly. Paul communicated God's heart to them:

> *You will be enriched in every way so that you*
> *can be generous on every occasion, and through*
> *us your generosity will result in thanksgiving to*
> *God.*
>
> 2 Corinthians 9:11

Their desire to be generous despite a lack of earthly resources released a promise from Heaven that He would make them financially rich so they could exercise even greater generosity and promote praise to God. True generosity should always generate the praise and thanks of those giving and those receiving. Both are equally blessed. This is a noteworthy Kingdom principle.

It's important to know that generosity cannot coexist with

poverty. If you are poverty-minded, you will withhold being generous to those who are truly needy.

> *If anyone is poor among your fellow Israelites in any of the towns of the land the* LORD *your God is giving you, do not be hardhearted or tightfisted toward them. Rather, be openhanded and freely lend them whatever they need.*
>
> Deuteronomy 15:7-8

Fear inhibits Generosity

A sign of poverty is a hardheartedness and stinginess. A closed fist refuses to give to those in need. Withholding generosity always signifies fear: *We believe we will lack if we give something away, so we hold on tightly to what we have.* Stinginess is the result, and His flow of blessing through us to others is stopped up; whereas, generosity opens the floodgates for rivers of blessing.

The Lord first started speaking to me about this when we lived in Fiji that summer where, as I mentioned before, we had to use much of our savings to live on. Nevertheless, we were at least able to care for our own needs, and our family enjoyed the experience of living in beautiful Fiji.

One day, when we were all out walking on the beach, my daughter asked, "Hey Dad! Can I have an ice cream cone?" Up to this time, the day-to-day tension of our financial situation was taking its toll on me, and I just wasn't in a good frame of mind at that moment. So at first I told her no, but then reluctantly bought her one. When I finished paying for it, the Lord said to me: "Keith, did you notice how afraid you have become—so tightfisted that you can't even be generous to your daughter for such a small thing as an ice cream cone?"

That word from the Lord hit with such conviction right to my core. It was only then that I realized fear had, indeed, crept in, keeping me bound up in my heart so that I refused to be generous even to the ones I dearly love. The more I held on trying to guard the little money I had left, the faster the money seemed to slip away and the more afraid I became. It was a very unpleasant cycle I knew I had to break.

I have taken to heart that word of the Lord so that I recognize now when I am coming under poverty's influence by fear manifesting in my life in some way. I feel my hand clenching in its tightfisted position and my thinking focuses on how I can hold on to what money I have, or I begin questioning whether I will make it through the present financial crisis. I feel my heart begin to shut down out of fear. That is how you can test to see if poverty is taking hold. In such times, ask yourself: *Is fear at the root of what is driving me to make these particular choices? Is it fear of lack, a fear of not having enough, or a fear of others taking from me what I need?* You can tell when your heart is shrinking, becoming incapacitated, and reluctant to give because you carefully put measures in place to guard what "little" you have. Remember, unrealistic fears will always exaggerate and lie about your situation. You may have an underlying fear that no more provision will be coming your way. That's an unrealistic fear right there.

When a person is reacting out of a place of poverty and lack, he tends to hoard what he has. That person fears there will not be enough, and so to secure what is his, he shuts off generosity. Some regions of the world are under this spirit. One way you can tell that a poverty spirit is prevalent over a geographical area is in the way they price things out. For instance, when I have stayed at hotels in some foreign nations, wireless service or even a simple continental breakfast were not included with the room. They consider those "extras" and you are billed accordingly. Now I know there are reasonable extra services beyond a standard room that require a charge, but I've discovered that in certain regions where a poverty spirit is firmly established, even the most basic amenities that normally should be free are not. An example of this is when you have to pay for toilet paper in public restrooms or even to use the toilet itself. These are indications that a spirit of poverty needs to be broken over an area.

As I've said, fear is at the root of poverty. Sometimes people are trying to get ahead in life and so they skimp and save everything they can but fail to realize they must have a correct heart attitude of generosity. As Proverbs says:

> *A generous person will prosper; whoever refreshes others will be refreshed.*

11:25

Generosity extended actually opens up a hundredfold return. Sometimes we have to give to break through the mentality that says, *If I give, I won't have what I need.*

Giving and receiving are both critical to becoming a healthy resource person. Some people are great at giving but terrible at receiving, and vice versa. Some people can give quite easily in one particular area, but are stingy and guarded in others. The key is to discover in what area the Lord wants to focus—giving or receiving—and prepare for an upgrade.

Feeling Obligated to Give

I spent years with the mindset that, because I was the pastor, I had to be the one who paid for everyone's meals when we went to a restaurant. In my mind, I was the generous one with the money because I had access to the church credit card and petty cash. But in reality, true generosity was not really coming from my heart. I was simply in charge of a designated fund which others did not have access to. It was an obligation on my part as pastor, and I knew it was expected of me in my church ministry. I felt pressured, though; whether it was self-initiated or it came from others, I'm not really sure, but it was definitely there.

This was really highlighted to me living seven years in the parsonage where we had many homeless stop through expressing a need for help—some with good motives, but others not. Sometimes we would give a blanket from our own home because that's all we had, but then as they walked away disappointed because we didn't give money, they cussed us out. That hurt. But others received our simple gift with genuine gratitude.

Living in a church house where people expected to get something from us whenever a need arose became an obligation that turned my generosity sour. I remember an incident when a parishioner in our church called one day and announced, "Hey, Keith! I have a guy here that I picked up and he needs a place to stay. Would you mind letting him stay at your house overnight?"

I knew that the parishioner calling owned his own home. *Why doesn't he take him to his own house to stay overnight with his family?* I wondered. *Why is he calling me?* But what could I say? As the pastor, I felt obliged once again to give sacrificially above and beyond anyone else in the church, because in my mind, this was *expected* of me. Reluctantly, I agreed to this request. I think back about how risky it was—allowing someone off the streets to stay in my home with my 2 young children. God protected and covered us, of course. But it only highlighted the struggles in my heart, and I knew God was calling me up to a higher journey to know genuine generosity. I desperately needed Him to soften my heart and change my attitude about giving with a demonstration of what it should look like.

When generosity is preached and giving is presented in an obligatory way, you don't know what is really in your heart until the expectation and pressure lifts. For instance, how much would you give in tithes and offerings if you knew that God would bless you anyway? How much would you give to a person in need if no one was looking? Matthew 6:3 addresses this:

> *But when you give to the needy, do not let your left hand know what your right hand is doing.*

What would you give if you knew no one would ever know what you gave? Would you give if there were no expectation to give or not to give? That's a good test to see where your heart is! Do you feel obligated to give or pay for something because you are the one with money? I didn't really know what was in my heart regarding giving and generosity until I stopped pastoring and no longer had the church credit card and petty cash fund at my disposal. In fact, later on I had no credit cards or extra cash to pool from. It is interesting to see how generosity is manifested in your life when you have few resources from which to draw. That, too, is a real test. Can you still give generously?

A Time to Receive . . .

I remember a few times in pastoring when I literally had no money and my cupboards were nearly depleted of food. Here I had moved into this new house and was living at a higher economic level that tapped all my available resources. I was still learning how to take this new ground of trusting God for more, but it required that my wife, Heather, get a different job. Up to that time, she had been working alongside of me at the church. Eventually, as she worked outside the church, it was a more prosperous season where we were able to save money and even had some extra.

But in this moment, finances were extremely tight. I had no extra whatsoever, and I had more bills than money coming in. I was crying out to the Lord one day, "Father! You know my situation!"

"Keith," He answered, "remember the people that offered to help you the last few months? I want you to humble yourself and take them up on their offers."

That sent me immediately into a wrestling match. "But Lord! . . . I can't do that." I felt like the manager in Luke who thought he'd have to beg:

> *The manager said to himself, "What shall I do now? My master is taking away my job. I'm not strong enough to dig, and **I'm ashamed to beg**."*
>
> 16:3, emphasis added

It felt like I was going to have to grovel, and I just couldn't do that. I had never before been in such a vulnerable financial spot. *Plus*, I thought, *how would it look? Lord! People will think I am not a good financial manager or something!*

But I really needed help . . . real bad. The needs at home were getting critical. I considered the two who offered to help me: One lived quite a distance away, and the other was my brother who lived in the same town as me and was a part of our church. I phoned up the person who lived far away and asked him for help. It was humbling, to say the least. He immediately asked his church to write a check and sent it to me. That was the very thing I had personally done in my own pastorate for many needy pastors, and we, as a church, had sown into many other churches. It gave me great pleasure to be able to do that for them. But to be on the receiving end . . . well, that was undoing me.

Then I phoned my brother . . . "I need your help," I told him. He was so gracious and understanding that both he and his wife came right over and brought us bags of groceries. I remember weeping with gratitude, but it was so humbling to be on the receiving end. It made me feel like my faith was too small so that I had to ask for help. *Am I really a man of God or not?* That's what I was feeling. The help I needed from others didn't make me feel like anyone's hero or the provider and resource of many, but rather, a needy person who lacked great faith. Wild and unreasonable thoughts raced through my head: *How could you say you are a man of great faith? Look at all these needs you have.* On and on went the accusatory questioning of my faith. But faith is not about the ability to never be in need where you must call on others to help you out. It is the ability to trust God for the full provision of those needs, whether your hands provide the means or whether you receive it as a gift from someone else. The fact is, both ways of receiving provision require faith. It requires faith to work and faith to receive. I am getting better at receiving.

Give with No Strings Attached

There have been times on the receiving end, however, when I have sensed there was a motive attached to the gift. I have asked myself at such times, *Is he trying to get a one up on me or is he genuinely giving this gift with no expectation of something in return?* I have had a number of instances as a pastor and traveling minister where a person's giving was truly a heart-felt expression of their generosity and I felt no strings attached whatsoever. But at other times, I very quickly discovered the real reason for their generosity was to gain easy access to my prophetic gifting. For this reason, I became very guarded when receiving a gift.

I received an invitation to meet up with someone I had just met. The Lord spoke clearly to my spirit: "Keith, just express your thanks for whatever you receive from him." That was it. I sensed it would be a substantial gift. When I met up with him and he presented his gift to me, my heart spilled over with gratitude. But I observed that I did not feel a sense of unworthiness as I usually did; there was no residual of an impoverished needy person. In fact, the whole experience was empowering as I sensed the pleasure of the Lord wanting to bless his son with a gift that was especially meaningful. I realized that receiving should be just as much a joy as giving when we learn that God wants to bless our socks off. If we feel like it's up to us to be the ones giving all the time, we need to ask ourselves, *Am I giving because it makes me feel important or is this genuine? Am I giving because I feel this is a way to earn love or to gain a place of influence?* That's an important question, because our motives to give can be to buy our favor with someone we look up to or need something from. The Scripture says:

> *A gift opens the way and ushers the giver into the presence of the great.*
>
> Proverbs 18:16

That's why it's good to ask ourselves when giving a gift, *Am I trying to get an open door for a connection I need, or solicit favor with someone, or am I genuinely giving this with a pure heart with no ulterior motives?* I observed as I was growing in my prophetic gifting that if I were to prophesy over someone, it would immediately boost our relationship. I could sense a new favor with them right away. If I didn't feel like I had any kind of rapport with a person and I was feeling a bit insecure, all I had to do was prophesy over them and the relationship would immediately open up. I was learning that my prophetic gifting had power and anointing and it genuinely touched people's lives. I knew that, like giving a costly gift, it could potentially open doors for me to minister in someone's church. The Lord began to work on my insecurities in this area by reassuring me of my value aside from my gift. I immediately made an adjustment so that when I was prophesying, if I felt any kind of neediness in the person receiving, any sense of insecurity, a fear of rejection by that person, or any concern that my refusal to prophesy would affect a potential open door for me, I refused to prophesy. This would ensure that my heart motives remained pure and would protect my gift from deception or falsehood.

True Motives

You may be thinking, "Well, yeah Keith. Isn't that obvious? I mean, the Bible clearly says not to use your gift like Balaam did for money. That's a no-brainer; anyone knows not to use his or her gifts that way." But the truth of the matter is many feel they won't be loved and accepted if they don't readily agree to such requests because they fear it will affect their connections in the future. They feel they have to beef up their relationships by giving, serving, and giving words of encouragement. They may feel like, they, as a person aside from their gift, aren't quite enough in the relationship. We learn very quickly that our gift can gain us entry to where we receive acceptance. It is similar to a person of means who suffers with a lack of self-worth and may unconsciously use his wealth to gain friends and connections.

Let me share something about needing to give. As I've said before, while giving and receiving are equally important, it is vitally important to know the motivation behind it. We are familiar with the story of Ananias and Sapphira. Within a context of a citywide revival, the hearts of the believers were moved to give to the growing church generously and sacrificially. Gifts were pouring in from all sources. Many were even selling their homes and lands and donating the money to the apostles for the work of the ministry. Ananias and Sapphira also sold some land but kept back a portion of the money from the sale for their personal use. There was nothing wrong with them doing this; it was, after all, their land to sell. What was wrong was that they wanted people to *believe* they were donating the full amount they sold it for, when, in fact, they weren't. The omission of the truth was deception and an intolerable lie.

> *Then Peter said, "Ananias, how is it that Satan has so filled your heart that you have lied to the Holy Spirit and have kept for yourself some of the money you received for the land? Didn't it belong to you before it was sold? And after it was sold, wasn't the money at your disposal? What made you think of doing such a thing? You have not lied to human beings but to God."*

> Acts 5:3-4

Ananias and Sapphira were more concerned that people saw them as extremely generous and so they lied about the portion they kept back for themselves, thinking they could deceive the apostles and the church. The cost for their deception was death. It was a sobering lesson for the new church of Jerusalem: God sees the heart and its true motives.

I went through a season where the Lord wanted me to grow in authentically giving from my heart. He wanted me to give generously because of what He was building in me, to be a wealthy resource. This was the time when I was no longer pastoring and could no longer depend upon church funds at my disposal to "give" and demonstrate how generous I was. Like I said, I had very little money and no credit cards whatsoever, so anything I gave would be coming out of a place of true sacrifice. It really tested my resolve to give generously. At the same time I was also working my way through the tensions of mounting bills on a small income where we were barely making it. Still the Lord insisted that I see myself as a wealthy resource, even though there was no visible proof of that reality, and He wanted me to go after it as a rich person would do. He was teaching me that I am not a victim of my circumstances because the Lord is always generous, always good, and has unlimited wealth and resources available to all who would access it. This was my mission and my goal in this season.

On occasion, I would go out to have a meal with my well-to-do friend. Most of the time, he would insist on paying for our meals. But as I began to break through into freedom in this area, I insisted on paying our bill. It wasn't that I had extra money to do this. I just knew that something bigger was happening in me and I needed to press right on through generously. I was beginning to believe that I was a resource even before it was manifested and so I functioned as a wealthy-minded person. I practiced living from the very place I was heading.

I began to declare aloud, "I need to give!" knowing it is for my own benefit. There was a wrestling in my heart, though. I inwardly resisted paying for others meals, desiring instead to be on the receiving end of a well-to-do person; but I knew I had to personally break through. When I first started insisting on paying the bill for our meal, my heart didn't enjoy it, because I was focused on the fear that there would not be enough financially. I knew I had to press through and be generous anyway to break the cycle of fear-motivated living and also press through the lie that kept telling me I was insignificant, poor, and powerless.

Breaking Obligation

One time I was ministering at another church in another state. I had been there before and was developing relationships with the leadership. I had gone out to dinner with the pastor and a businessman on his leadership team who was a part of his church. When it came time to pay for the meal, the businessman paid for the meal. But something didn't feel right. I sensed there was an underlying obligation for him to pay for our meals—some kind of veiled pressure from the pastor.

Following the meal, I was riding with the businessman back to his house where I was staying and said, "Thank you for paying for the meal. How much was it, may I ask?"

He told me what he paid and I felt impressed to give him the money to cover the expense. This really surprised him, and initially he refused, but at my insistence, he accepted it. It only confirmed what I had been sensing.

"It's always expected that I will pay for the meals," he told me. In our conversations over the next few days, I learned that he was expected to pay for the honorarium of guest speakers. I went after his motivation behind why he agrees to do this, knowing that it was under coercion, and challenged him to only give out of a willing heart. If he didn't want to give, I instructed, then he shouldn't! In so doing, however, it occurred to me that my honorarium could be substantially affected, and I had hoped what I took home from this particular meeting would help give my family a good Christmas. Nevertheless, it was more needful to help this man make the adjustment necessary in the motives of his giving.

The pastor decided on his own to take an offering for me at the service, something he didn't normally do. The amount, as I expected, was substantially less than an honorarium would have been had the businessman provided his usual. But I did right to challenge him on his motives of giving, and because he didn't know where he stood, he decided not to give that day. When the pastor handed me the check, he jokingly said to me, "If you hadn't had that conversation with my business guy, the amount would have been more!" I knew this was partially true, but I felt like I had won a victory with the Lord that weekend. The bigger issue at stake in this situation was, *How would I respond with what God revealed through my prophetic gift? Would I be quiet about the wrong motives that I sensed knowing it could adversely impact me personally, or would I speak up and deal with it?* By His grace, I passed the test!

A month or so later, an unexpected check came in the mail from that same businessman. He sent me the amount that made up for much of the difference that had been lacking from the church offering. In the end, God made sure I didn't suffer financial loss because I had been obedient to His word. His rewards are sure to come.

Several things happened in this incident. First, I was learning how to be a giver whether it was comfortable or not. Second, I was learning not to allow what seemed to be a generous act keep me from questioning improper motives. I was beginning to break free of poverty in this area by giving at a time when I needed someone else's generosity, and giving even when it hurt. It helped me understand how true generosity gives sacrificially.

God Sees Your Sacrificial Giving

A generous gift can be an opportunity to demonstrate how a person really cares for those in need and it also opens up the heavens to respond with favorable return blessings. Cornelius was a great example of such generosity.

> *The angel answered, "Your prayers and gifts to the poor have come up as a memorial offering before God."*

Acts 10:4b

The Lord sent an angel to Cornelius, a non-Jew, to deliver this message. Simultaneously, God told Peter in an open vision to go to the Gentiles and bring the message of the gospel. Up till this time, there wasn't any work among non-Jews because the Jews believed Gentiles were unclean, and therefore, out of reach of redemption. Cornelius' generosity to the poor and needy of his community opened up something in the spirit realm that caused God to respond. Since God knows the motives of the heart, we can trust when we get in proper sync with the motives of giving and receiving, we will receive Heaven's blessing. When it is time to give, we will receive blessing, and when it is time to receive, we will receive blessing. Either way, we will be blessed, even in difficult circumstances, when we give out of a pure heart.

When God sees our sacrifice of generosity with a true motive of love for others, He is genuinely moved.

And do not forget to do good and to share with others, for with such sacrifices God is pleased.

Hebrews 13:16

The sacrifice of sharing what we have with others pleases the Lord, and He will repay those who take care of the poor and needy.

Free to Give, Healed to Receive

When we give from a heart of true motives toward the care of others, and when we receive a gift with a genuine heart of thanks because we see the Lord's goodness, we are positioning ourselves for sustainable blessings in our lives. You know you are truly free of poverty when you can receive a gift with thanks and not feel unworthy. You also know you are free of poverty when you can give out of pure joy with no strings attached or false motivation. You can even ask for help when you need it, free from a poverty spirit and released from the weight of lack. The ability to ask others for help is actually a sign of health in your life. Wealthy people have no problem asking for what they need because they know that when they ask, they'll receive what they need. People who see themselves as valuable speak up for what they need. This is a healthy way to live.

After four years of living in a rental home, I began the arduous process of trying to buy a house. The Lord gave us wonderful favor to offer a purchase price we could afford. Even still, we needed the downpayment that would be due in 30 days! We had saved up and had a good portion of it, but still came up short for the full amount.

Several months before, a friend had offered to give me some money to get a much-needed second vehicle. At the time he offered to sow into this need, we couldn't find the car we needed for the amount he was offering, so we held off accepting his gift. During this 30-day period of the house purchase, I asked if he would consider putting the money towards the downpayment of the house instead of the car purchase. I explained the situation, and as I did, I realized I was having the conversation with him feeling no guilt or shame whatsoever. Whether he gave the money or not was not even the issue anymore. The breakthrough for me was the fact that I could even have that conversation! I knew I wasn't groveling for help because of feeling powerless. Quite the contrary, I felt *powerful,* knowing God was my true source, and if this wasn't the way He wanted to supply, then I would anticipate His provision in some other way. But if my friend was able to give toward this need, I would be joyful and grateful, and if not, my relationship with him would remain as amiable as always. Though my friend was in a tight place financially, he graciously and sacrificially gave towards the downpayment of the house. Thank God for his generous decision and help! And God was happy with mine, as well, so it was a win-win. There is great peace when you begin to see the transforming work in your heart and its healthy motives in giving and receiving.

Breaking free to walk in healthy giving and receiving makes for a powerful person indeed. And it takes a powerful person to develop their life and resources to a place that produces abundance for them to prosper well.

In the next chapter, I want to talk about how to recognize the difference between a wealthy-kingly mindset and a poverty-pauper mindset.

QUESTIONS TO PONDER

1. Do you have a hard time being generous? What are the reasons?

_____

_____

_____

2. Do you have a hard time receiving? Describe why that is.

_____

_____

_____

3. Name those people from whom you can easily receive. Why? What kinds of things are easy for you to you receive? Explain.

_____

_____

_____

_____

4. In what situations do you release generosity easily? Why?

_____

_____

5. Identify any wrong motives you may have in giving or receiving. What would an upgrade look like?

_____

_____

_____

_____

Nine

THINK LIKE A KING

The mindset of a king concerns himself with long-term goals toward his big dreams with the hopes of leaving behind a legacy long after he is gone. Whereas a poverty-mindset is preoccupied with the concerns and needs of today: *How do I get a meal on the table, get the bills paid, and make it through another day?* Weighed down in such a way, it is impossible for him to even dream of getting out of his situation, let alone aspire to his God-given destiny of greatness.

When all your energy is spent thinking and worrying about the bills that need to be paid, you're unable to think creatively about your future. Even your prayers are preoccupied with pressing needs so that you cannot see God's greater dreams. I have traveled to many countries and have observed that the most some people can dream about is a roof over their head and how to put food on the table. The biggest dream they can come up with is owning their own home one day, working at a better job, and giving their children the best education. While those are all good aspirations, God is setting our sights far beyond our daily needs. It's definitely a good start to move out of impoverished thinking, but to truly be free, you must think much higher and greater. I have come to understand that in order for that to happen, people need *hope*; they need a vision of something greater in order to dream, because it is hope that sustains you as you pursue your God-dream.

An Inherited Mindset

I grew up in a church environment with a shortsighted system and no big dreams. Yet I held big dreams in my heart . . . dreams to preach to scores of people in stadiums, travel the world and ignite revival fires, etc. But I lived in a small church culture where spirituality meant being content with living near the poverty level; in such pitiful conditions big dreams can never be realized. It hurt me to see my grandparents consumed with worry most of their lives about where their next dollar would come from. It also pained me to see my parents constantly struggling through one financial difficulty after another. A division formed in my thinking: Greatness and poverty cannot work hand in hand; one will eventually overthrow the other. You can't achieve destiny in poverty, neither can you stay in poverty and pursue your out-of-the-box big dreams. One has to go. For me personally, poverty had to go. This was the first step towards breaking free of this restrictive mindset. I had to recognize that I had been living under a mentality of scarcity, barely getting by.

I didn't realize that I had inherited a poverty mentality until after my pastorate ended. I began to see what a crippling effect the church system of tithing had on me. I had become captive to the mercy of people's giving at church to determine the extent of our financial potential. Sometimes, we were okay; other times we were barely able to pay salaries. I had no mindset other than to convince church members to give more money. You can see what a limiting effect that system can have on a person when their only source of finances is from the tithes of church members and offerings of attendees. What is that attitude going to produce in someone? It will manifest in control and manipulation that persuades and pressures people for what you need, and worry and anxiety about what will happen if they don't come through. This same mentality is pervasive in other areas as well and keeps people locked in impoverished thinking. For instance, those who have given in to poverty may look only to governmental and/or social assistance programs worrying if and when they'll receive much-needed financial aid. Some may resort to blaming their own personal loss and suffering on others instead of recognizing that they carry a victim mindset that keeps them in a cycle of bondage. The truth is, Jesus in His goodness wants to shake off anything that isn't of the Kingdom or isn't founded on a heavenly mindset. No matter our situation, He always positions us to prosper in everything.

Much of the time, jealousy and anger come out of the fear that someone else has power over me, or they possess something I wish I had, or they have favor with someone that I don't have access to. These kinds of thoughts expose a lack mentality. It says: *There is not enough to go around.* Some may target their anger at their nation's leader, the government, a spouse or relative, their boss, church elder, co-workers, friends or neighbors—you name it. It all stems from the same mentality that says: *I am not powerful; they are. They need to help me out here. I hope they can see how pitiful my condition is and give me what I need!* Self-pity is simply a sign of someone who has been rendered powerless because they lost the hope to believe they are able to change their circumstances.

Negative Circumstances Shape Mindsets

In the movie, "Gladiator," Maximus, who once was the great general of the armies of Rome, was in prison and was forced to continue to perform as a gladiator under the threat of death. The new Emperor had put him in this place and he had it out for him. In one scene, Maximus was asked what needed to be done in the government to turn evil around. "The answer is to have the Emperor killed," he said.

"Oh Maximus," came the reply, "you used to be such a different thinker. What happened to you?"

Life's hardships had reduced Maximus from a powerful man to a victim who felt helpless to his circumstances. The only solution he could see to his hopeless situation was, *Get rid of the guy who did this.* The narrow focus on his bitter condition limited his ability to see what needed to happen for the future of his nation.

Sometimes we get stuck in the here-and-now crisis with its urgent needs and can settle into a similar way of thinking. How does that happen? We lose hope, and so the only plausible answer is to pressure the people who have what we need to give us what we're desperate for. *If I can communicate to them in a convincing way,* we say, *then perhaps they'll help us out and give us what we need.* In reality, we need to realize something within ourselves needs to change. People are not our servants or our masters. We cannot make demands on people with a sense of entitlement that compels them to meet our needs. Instead we must honor and value them recognizing that ultimately, God is in complete control of it all. 1 Peter 2:17 says:

*Show proper respect to everyone, love the family
of believers, fear God, honor the emperor.*

Wholehearted Devotion

God can move people on our behalf even when conditions appear to be hopeless with no obvious help. A great example of this is the prophet Daniel. He didn't seem to be in the best of circumstances. He was an exiled Jew who had been conscripted to work for the pagan king of the most powerful and influential empire of his day. Daniel didn't choose his job role or position, but was specifically selected because of his unique skills. Several times he faced the threat of death because of evil accusations and threats, but through it all, God remained the only one he bowed to and his prayers to Heaven continued unceasing. He refused to surrender or conform to the idolatrous culture demands of "progressive" spirituality. Though he stayed true to his integrity, he was still thrown into the lion's den. But Daniel knew his God, and he was assured of his rescue because he trusted Him wholeheartedly. The result of Daniel's exclusive faith and devotion to God is that the ruler of the most powerful earthly kingdom encountered the greater, the Kingdom of God Almighty.

Learning to Trust God as My Source

As I said earlier, the Lord was working with me to be free of dependency upon people as my financial source while pastoring my church. When we entered into a spiritual renewal back in the late nineties, a group of people who were a part of the solid fabric of the church began resisting the free moving of the Spirit. They were offended by the direction we were going and threatened to leave our church. At that time these individuals provided our primary financial support.

One day some of the discontented members said to me, "We want the old Keith back, and if that doesn't happen, we are going to leave this church . . . and take our finances elsewhere!" My mind was immediately filled with worrisome thoughts about what that would be like. But I knew I couldn't return to the person I used to be, and so, true to their word, they left the church. Following their exit, the church suffered financially. During that season, God began teaching us that He could sustain the church even without their tithes. One month, we received donations outside of the church in the exact amount of money we needed for staff salaries. These donors knew nothing of the difficulties we were facing at that time. The amount that came in that month was exactly the same amount we would have normally received from the church tithes to cover our expenses. God was, indeed, showing Himself faithful and capable of taking care of us regardless who gave that month or didn't give. We did not have to give in to unreasonable demands or be held hostage by financial manipulation of a few. In choosing to fully follow His Spirit, our faith was enlarged with this vivid example that He alone is our Source!

Another time, the largest giver in our church began to have a serious disagreement with the direction of the church leadership and threatened to pull his finances if we didn't change what we were doing. We definitely needed his money, but I was more intent on keeping the fear of the Lord in my life than cowering with the fear of man. I maintained our position in a loving but firm manner despite his threat and trusted God for any consequential result. As always, He faithfully sustained us through that time.

During the renewal, we were pressing in to receive all God had for us. Some folks got offended and left the church. Those who stayed continued to receive blessings from Heaven and miracles resulted, including a lady who was healed of cancer!

She was so blessed by this that she gave a significant donation to our church, which actually paid the salaries of my staff and myself, just when our finances were about to go in the red. We watched God encourage us in the tough times, building up our faith time and again.

Lessons of a Desert Journey

Though it was a season of blessing and refreshing, it felt more like the desert that the ancient Israelites experienced. God's primary lessons were teaching us to trust Him for our daily provision and each incident caused us to see Him as the sole provider of all good things. It also taught me that I live for God's approval, not men, and that He will ultimately sustain and provide for me. I knew that if He was capable of commanding the ravens to feed Elijah, He certainly was able to take care of me.

Like any good season, if you don't continue to advance in a forward movement, however, you may find yourself incapacitated and ill equipped for the next season. The Israelites were meant to take the lessons of trusting the Lord for their daily bread in the desert so that they would have the internal values built in as they entered and possessed the Promised Land. But life in their new location would require an entirely different skill set. No longer would they get an easy provision of manna dropped out of Heaven for their daily bread; they would now have to possess the things they needed and desired in the full confidence of knowing He had given them the Land for the taking.

I feel like so many people have floundered in the desert for too many years when the Lord is offering them to move on ahead and take their Promised Land. So often I see pastors and ministry leaders too attached to the church-tithe system that it often immobilizes them. In one season, it was easy manna from Heaven, but in the next season, it was barely enough. We need way more than barely enough in order to possess our promised land!

A whole different set of spiritual muscles is needed to acquire your dreams. That is why the Lord told Joshua again and again as he was preparing to enter the Promised Land, "Be strong and very courageous."[9] He was certainly going to need it.

I didn't realize that receiving my income from church tithes would eventually disable me to think creatively about generating wealth for myself and instead cause me to rely on others for what I needed. On the one hand, I had learned valuable lessons in trusting the Lord's daily provision even with opposition and threats that radically reduced the tithes and offerings. But on the other hand, I had functioned somewhat like a beggar with my hands out hoping people would see my need and drop a few spare coins. In some ways, I became dependent upon the goodwill of people for provision.

But the Lord was changing all that. In His goodness, the only way I could build faith muscles in this area was to stop taking a church salary altogether. Learning to develop my own resources was a part of my journey out of expecting others to give me money as payment for a job I completed. As I began to step into a whole new way of acquiring income, I also developed an expanded vision of what was available. For so long, it was like I had been fishing in a small pond, but when I expanded my vision to see other possibilities, I realized there were numerous well-stocked and abundant lakes of provision to fish from. Not only that, I was no longer restricted to just fish with a single pole; I could learn how to net a large harvest.

Throw Your Net on the Other Side

One of those abundant lakes was a new country that opened up to me. The summer after I left Fiji, the Lord said, "Keith, throw your net on the other side."

"Where?" I asked, and He indicated a specific nation. I had no connection with that nation at the time, but six months later I received an invitation. Ministering in that nation became a starting point where I learned my heavenly value and worth in wages. No longer did I bring in a barely-enough wage; now it was a generous portion—a wage not dependent merely upon my gifts and skills, but based on His lavish goodness. God directed me on a clear path out of the desert of focused searching for my daily provision and into the land of milk-and-honey abundance. I had told the Lord in Fiji I would no longer do ministry with a lack of finances such as I had encountered there. So He moved me from the desert of lack into His Promised Land of supernatural abundance where powerful, hope-filled people thrive.

The Church is in a major shift today of moving into that Promised Land of abundance. It requires a whole different way of living life, that's for sure. Look at some of these differences in the following Scripture.

The land you are entering to take over is not like the land of Egypt, from which you have come, where you planted your seed and irrigated it by foot as in a vegetable garden. But the land you are crossing the Jordan to take possession of is a land of mountains and valleys that drinks rain from heaven. It is a land the LORD your God cares for; the eyes of the LORD your God are

continually on it from the beginning of the year
to its end.

Deuteronomy 11:10-12

God wants to give us a land that *He* will water. The rains are His responsibility, and in its season, the dry ground is well saturated to receive new seed and nurture its growth. The Promised Land isn't a land to be worked by the sweat of our brow, nor is it a desert with daily manna, sufficient only for a single day. Rather, it is a well-watered garden of lavish provisions, more than we could ever envision, even in our wildest dreams.

But we must go after our big dreams if we want to see them fulfilled. So, I'm urging you . . . step out . . . go for it, and as you move forward step by step, become the resource that is needed. Possessing your dreams (like possessing the Promised Land) requires that you live empowered and stay proactive. When you begin to pursue and possess your dreams—seeing way beyond your daily needs—you are well on your way to becoming a person of royalty and thinking like a king.

In the next chapter, I want to explore what it means to possess your Promised Land, that land of dreams.

QUESTIONS TO PONDER

1. Do you know that there is a great land of provision waiting for you to enter in? What is it?

_____

_____

2. Are you stuck in a small world of drudgery, laboring to meet your daily needs or working in a frustrating dead-end salaried position that feels more like a dry arid place? If so, what would your promised-land dream job look like?

_____

_____

3. What do you think are some of the first steps you can take towards your promised land and a different way of generating income? List some ideas to explore these.

_____

_____

_____

_____

_____

4. What do you see as potential hindrances to keeping you from pursuing your dream(s)? List them out.

_____

_____

_____

_____

5. Do you have testimonies of God's faithfulness in a desert season where God was teaching you valuable lessons? List these. What do you believe He was preparing you for through those challenges?

_____

_____

_____

_____

_____

_____

_____

Ten

SMALL BEGINNINGS FUEL MOMENTUM

*Y*ou already possess the keys to becoming a resource, but you have to start somewhere. In order to discover what those resources are, a good first step is to take an assessment of your gifts and skills, callings, passions, possessions, big dreams and creative ideas, etc., and then identify the seed to start with.

In our society, people often look for the easy road, the quick fix, the fast track to wealth and fame through a big-winning lottery ticket, the lucky number, or a surprise inheritance that suddenly comes to rescue them out of their financial misery or helps to launch their big dream. While God does surprise us with unexpected blessings in possessions, finances, salary increases and job advancements, those who don't know how to steward the assets they already have will certainly not be able to handle a large windfall. Studies have shown that many who win the lottery end up broke after a few years. And, some who have built beautiful houses or spent big money on remodeling such as seen on the "Extreme Home Makeover" TV program, often end up foreclosing because they had not learned effective resource management.

For this reason God most often upgrades our life gradually. I'd like to suggest the Kingdom principle of "little by little".

> *The LORD your God will drive out those nations before you, **little by little** . . .*
>
> Deuteronomy 7:22a, emphasis added

Giving careful attention to strategic management of what God gives is preparation for the wealth of abundance He intends in our future. We first must steward the little well. Proverbs 12:11 says:

> *Those who work their land will have abundant food, but those who chase fantasies have no sense.*

A necessary first step is to work our "land" with the expectation of the abundance God is sending. Those who do not implement wise management with what has been given to them and set their priorities accordingly, will be unable to sustain a financial increase, whether expected or unforeseen.

Financially Trustworthy

As I said earlier, there is a difference between working

for money and money working for you. Many people are hard workers, but unfortunately, they do not experience increase. The goal is not necessarily to work harder, but to work *smarter*. Before we can be trusted with true riches, we must demonstrate we are trustworthy with the wealth of this world.

> *So if you have not been trustworthy in handling worldly wealth, who will trust you with true riches?*
>
> Luke 16:11

If we want to be entrusted with increasing His Kingdom, we must be ever maturing in our ability to be good stewards of all our earthly resources. That means we are taking on the skills necessary to properly manage our valuable assets (i.e., salary, bank account, possessions, house, car, etc.), no matter how small or insignificant it seems. The same is true for our skills and talents: invest them wisely and seek to increase them. Each material and spiritual asset we have is a blessing from God and an opportunity to demonstrate how we value it by taking good care of it. What we do today with our resources will be an investment toward our future potential.

A great example of this is Joseph. He had to demonstrate he was trustworthy in Potiphar's house and with the prison guard before he could be entrusted with saving Egypt from starvation during a severe famine. Each one of those opportunities was a stepping-stone in preparing him for greater stewardship and higher levels of wisdom. God gives this wisdom to those who steward His resources well and have proven themselves faithful and dependable.

We find another example in David's life. Before he was given the kingdom to rule, he first had to manage a few sheep. God carefully observed him in the small tasks of sheepherding and then anointed him to shepherd His beloved people as their future king. Here's how God singled him out above all the others:

> *But the LORD said to Samuel, "Do not consider his appearance or his height, for I have rejected him. The LORD does not look at the things people look at. People look at the outward appearance, but the LORD looks at the heart."*

1 Samuel 16:7

Faithfulness Brings Advancement

God was looking for faithfulness and integrity, a heart of worship and courage, and he found it in David. Notice he didn't promote him to the royal court as king that very day. No, David had to be prepared for this assignment of governing God's people through a series of tests and trials . . . little by little. First, he took out the national enemy, Goliath. Second, he went to work for the king as a minstrel and then became his bodyguard. Later on he led armies for many years under the rulership of the king. And finally, after many years hiding out and being pursued by the king as an enemy, he was promoted to the throne. Through it all, and in each small advancement, David remained faithful to God. Understanding the process and embracing the training along the way is key to long-term success.

Once you discover and understand the gifts that are within you, the next step in the process is growing your resources. The same principle that applies to stewarding your life circumstances also applies to stewarding your talents. So many people have a dream of having more, being someone who rises to greatness, following their heart's passion, but they're often not prepared for the long arduous process to get there. I want to share the story of my wife's journey into becoming a resource with the hope that it will awaken the desire within you to take the first steps toward your own dream.

See the Need

Heather's journey first started in Brazil, where she spent six weeks away from home to live in the slums of Brazil to be a part of Heidi Baker's school. It was life-changing for her, to say the least. One day, she saw a group of children and women making jewelry in the streets. They were huddled over their crafts, working hurriedly in a very hush-hush manner. Curious about what they were doing Heather asked one of the locals about it because something didn't feel right.

"They are a part of the slave trade," she was told. The women and children were making jewelry just to stay alive. Even though they had to work under such harsh conditions, it assured them that they would be fed, cared for, and protected.

Heather's heart was pricked when she learned this, and the Lord said to her, "What are you going to do about this?"

"Lord, what can I do?" she replied. "It is such a huge problem and I wouldn't even know where to begin!" She didn't receive an immediate answer but sensed God would show her in time.

Invest Your Seed Wisely

About three years passed and one day the Lord said, "Heather, now is the time to start doing something about what I showed you in Brazil!"

Again she asked, "Lord! But what can I do?" He then instructed her to begin by taking two paintings she had just finished and sell them. Surprisingly, they sold for two hundred dollars. It wasn't a lot of money, but it was the seed.

Then the Lord said, "Now take that two hundred dollars and go to L.A. and buy some jewelry." There she found a market of artisans from poor nations selling their wares. Following that, she got a business license and called her business, "Accessorize Your World." On one of our next ministry trips together, Heather began selling the jewelry, and as it sold, she bought more to increase her inventory. The concept was to help artisans living in poverty by providing viable opportunities to sell their crafts in order to create sustainable income.

When starting a business, much of the income needs to be reinvested back into the business—especially at the beginning. You have to be careful not to "eat" your seed. The challenge when you need money is to reinvest that money to make more money. But if you take your money and use it on living expenses instead of sowing it back into the business, you won't have the necessary increase for growth and advancement. Momentum forward will be lost.

Heather soon developed a business plan, a mission statement and vision, along with new connections for her business and ministry. Soon people began to call her from all over. It was amazing to see this begin to happen shortly after it was publicized. A few people from foreign nations contacted her: "Hey, we have someone in this country making jewelry. Would you like to see a few samples?" And so, her ministry and desire to help the very poor by selling their crafts continued to grow.

Then she stumbled onto Fair Trade. She didn't even know

that Fair Trade was very similar to her own mission of helping the poor create sustainable income. She also discovered a market of businesses and brokers who buy handmade crafts, beads, jewelry, purses, etc., from international artisans just as she had been doing. So, Heather began to also buy from these artisans through this particular market who were selling handcrafted items from India, Africa, Fiji, the Philippines, and others. Her ultimate goal was that these artisans would be able to sell their product and thereby increase their household income, assuring them of a better life.

While we lived in Fiji, Heather encouraged a group of ladies who were a part of our supernatural school to develop artistic crafts based on their culture and representative of their nation. One Fijian woman took Heather's encouragement seriously and did just that. A very quiet but powerful leader who had attended our first supernatural school, she arose in the school to confront cultural norms that said women did not have a voice. By the end of the school, she had developed a very strong identity over her life. When she declared who she was publicly as God saw her, the anointing was tangible.

This woman began hand-painting Fijian wedding dresses, typical of their culture, and sold them for $150 to $200 dollars apiece. That was a month's wages! This simple craft completely revolutionized her family's economy. With the profits, she was also able to put her special-needs son into a specialized school. This is a vivid example of how God will take a simple desire and transform a family or people group through practical means.

On one of the return trips, this Fijian artisan invited Heather over to her house. She had never had a westerner in her house before so it was a big deal. She kept telling Heather how simple the dinner would be, but the truth is, she cooked up a feast and Heather was treated like royalty. She shared with Heather how the training had been a tremendous influence on her and the others.

"Don't look at the 20 students that attended the schools and think you didn't make a great impact," she told Heather that night. "My family and many others have been transformed by the teachings and interactions we had with you and the other teachers from The Mission!" We praise the Lord for such a great testimony. Hers was the first of many such testimonies to come: Lives transformed by the revelation of God's goodness, a change of personal identity, and the discovery of a resource buried deep within that just needed the key to access it. This is the blessing of investing what we have in the lives of others.

Start Small

I shared this story as an illustration of how you too can become a resource. It always starts small—sometimes with the smallest seed. But the most sustainable businesses or ministries are built little by little, consistently over time. Throughout Scripture we find that all God needed for a miracle was something small to work with. In the Kingdom, when you give away one loaf of bread, you get two in its place. That principle defies natural law and is worth discovering! If you want to see an increase, you have to understand Kingdom principles. When you give, sow, and work with even the smallest seed, all the while resisting discouragement at its seeming insignificance, you *will* see an increase. Zechariah 4:10 says:

> *For who has despised the day of small things?*
> *For these seven rejoice to see the plumb line in*
> *the hand of Zerubbabel . . . (NKJV)*

What was the Lord saying here? As you begin something significant, don't underestimate its small beginnings. The little bit is enough for God to transform it to something big! When you rejoice over the small things, you will experience increase and rejoice in the greater. Jesus understood this Kingdom principle.

Then some boats from Tiberias landed near the place where the people had eaten the bread after the Lord had given thanks.

John 6:23

When Jesus gave thanks for a few small loaves of bread and a couple of fish, the whole lot multiplied. Look around you right now. You have enough! You simply have to find out what to do with what you have. It's that simple. The first step of course, is to give thanks for what you already have. Then, declare: "Thanks, Dad! With You, I always have more than enough."

What's in Your Hand?

Once you have thanked God, find out what He wants you to do with what is in your hand, just as the Lord instructed Heather to take her two paintings and go sell them. Once she did that, she had what she needed to begin. So, I ask you, what do you have in your hand right now? What do you already have in your possession that you haven't even thought would be useful or profitable? Ask God to help you find the answer.

The prophet Elisha understood this Kingdom principle. One of the prophets that was part of his ministry died, and his wife contacted Elisha for help. In response, Elisha prompts her to take action.

Elisha replied to her, "How can I help you? Tell me, what do you have in your house?"

"Your servant has nothing there at all," she said,
"except a small jar of olive oil."

2 Kings 4:2

Notice that he asked her to take an inventory of what she had in her house—something he could work with. God always asks us to consider what we have to work with. Whether it is faith for a miracle, bread for multiplication, money for sowing, or talents to use and multiply, He needs something you already have to begin. The second step to becoming a resource is recognizing that you have something in your possession worth using and profitable. It may be an idea, a skill, a song, a gift, a possession, or even a character quality. Take inventory of what you already have, no matter how small or insignificant it may seem. Then once you've identified what it is, offer it fully to God.

For the next step, watch what Elisha tells the woman to do with a little bit of oil:

Elisha said, "Go around and ask all your neighbors for empty jars. Don't ask for just a few. Then go inside and shut the door behind you and your sons. Pour oil into all the jars, and as each is filled, put it to one side."

v 3-4

Elisha helped this widow discover what she could do with what little she had. She had a bit of oil. That was all. He told her she needed to go borrow some clay vessels from her neighbors. That would take some boldness on her part. Then she was to take the little bit of oil she had and pour it into those empty jars she had borrowed. Here is the next key: If you want to see an increase, it is going to take a leap of faith. Not only that, but you are going to have to *ask* for help, and that will take humility and courage on your part.

Take some time to consider one of the things that came to mind of what you have in your hand, and how it could be turned into something tangible and useful for others. Ask yourself: *How could I make this into a product that is profitable?* Ask God for some creative ideas. Ask your friends for help as well. They may have some great ideas to help identify what you have and how to offer it as a viable product.

Then you are going to have to put your product where it can be multiplied. If you are a singer but you've never let anyone hear your song, then how will God increase it? Have you thought about recording it and uploading it to iTunes? There are so many options for people who are just starting out to get their talent or product developed, produced, advertised, and then made available to the public. There are numerous channels to promote your new product through the Internet, social media, Ebay, Amazon.com, YouTube, etc., that will make it readily available and easy to find what you are offering.

God was involved in the widow's multiplication miracle since He gave Elisha the spirit of wisdom to know what to do with the oil and then increased its volume supernaturally once they filled the jars. This was indeed a miraculous act of God since the oil didn't run out until the last jar was full. Those who write songs, books, blogs, or paint, draw, play an instrument, bake, or make crafts find a creative idea that will continue to make them money again and again. It will sustain them. It doesn't take a lot; you simply use what you *already have* and find the place where it is best suited. All of this requires faith and courage to step out and put your resources out there so they can increase. It is your natural and God's supernatural ability merged together that produces the miracle. Your gift and God's wisdom for where the gift should go, as well as the grace to multiply it when it gets there, makes way for supernatural abundance.

The Breath of God is in What You are Using

Maybe you want to be a preacher to the nations, but you don't even have one opportunity. Meanwhile, take a sermon, which is your oil, and start giving it away. An idea might be to do a 5-minute YouTube clip or make it available on social media. Give it away to a youth group or whatever door is open to you. Define it and refine it until the door opens beyond your present borders into the nations. As you develop it faithfully, it will grow. God will only breathe on something that you are already using. He can't blow on something that isn't in use or that you've hidden away waiting for a "better" opportunity.

In Luke 19, the Lord rebukes the servant who doesn't use what was given him.

Then another servant came and said, "Sir, here is your mina; I have kept it laid away in a piece of cloth. I was afraid of you, because you are a hard man. You take out what you did not put in and reap what you did not sow."

His master replied, "I will judge you by your own words, you wicked servant! You knew, did you, that I am a hard man, taking out what I did not put in, and reaping what I did not sow? Why then didn't you put my money on deposit, so that when I came back, I could have collected it with interest?"

vs 20-23

This is not meant to frighten us to action but encourage us to activate what God has already given us and put it to good use.

From Begging to Beginnings

I have noticed that when people beg God to rescue them from their circumstances, He asks them, "What's in your hand?" Do you remember that incident with Moses leading the Israelites? They were really in a tight spot. They had just broken free of Pharaoh's tyranny and marched out from under Egyptian bondage where they had lived for generations. But in order to get to a place of freedom and a new beginning, the Israelites had to cross the Red Sea directly before them in order to evade the Egyptian elite force on a furious chase to recapture their slaves.

If you think that getting free of poverty is going to be easy, you are mistaken. The devil loves to keep people who profess the name of Jesus locked up in the bondage of lack. They make it to Heaven, but they don't take much territory on earth because of a poverty spirit. When you step into your dreams and destiny, you have to know that you are going to need a lot of perseverance to get you to the place of your dreamland—that place where money is working for you and you are living with a sustainable income.

Meanwhile, back at the edge of the Red Sea, the Israelites could see Pharaoh's army quickly gaining an advantage and inching ever closer. Their demise seemed sure. With nowhere to go and in utter terror, they begged God for rescue. Some call this prayer; God calls it a lack of faith.

> *Then the LORD said to Moses, "Why are you crying out to me? Tell the Israelites to move on. Raise your staff and stretch out your hand over the sea to divide the water so that the Israelites*

can go through the sea on dry ground. I will harden the hearts of the Egyptians so that they will go in after them. And I will gain glory through Pharaoh and all his army, through his chariots and his horsemen. The Egyptians will know that I am the LORD when I gain glory through Pharaoh, his chariots and his horsemen."

Exodus 14:15-18

From Rescue to Partnership

Moses did his best to encourage the Israelites that God would fight for them.

Moses answered the people, "Do not be afraid. Stand firm and you will see the deliverance the LORD will bring you today. The Egyptians you see today you will never see again. The LORD will fight for you; you need only to be still."

vs 13, 14

God had told the Israelites to leave Egypt, and He would take care of the rest.

"Not exactly correct, Moses," God interrupted his panicked prayers. "Why are you crying out to Me? What's that in your hand?"[10]

While Moses was waiting for God to do something, God was waiting for Moses. It's as if God is saying, "Yo . . . Mo! Dude! You are way more powerful than you realize. What you need to win is something you already possess; it's been there all along. You're My voice and My hands extended on the earth, so step up to the plate and hit one out of the park!"

Like Moses, more often than not, we are waiting for God to *do* something in our dire situation while all along He is waiting for *us* to do something. Once we start doing something with what we have, then God steps in and takes it to the next level.

So Moses looked at his hand, stretched it way out, and God parted the waters.

> *Then Moses stretched out his hand over the sea, and all that night the LORD drove the sea back with a strong east wind and turned it into dry land. The waters were divided, and the Israelites went through the sea on dry ground, with a wall of water on their right and on their left.*

vs 21-22

When you step out with what you have, then God begins to partner with you. But it isn't until you do something that God can do something. Proverbs says it like this:

> *In their hearts humans plan their course, but the LORD establishes their steps.*

16:9

When we step out with what is in our heart to do, bringing along the talents and abilities we have to work with, the Lord will arrange situations and order our steps that cause those desires and dreams to be realized.

Uncovering the Buried Treasure

You and I are not called to leave any talents buried or untapped when our life is over. Rather, we are called to work, advance, expand, and develop all the talents and abilities He has given us until we have the goal of a hundredfold return. A *hundredfold* is the goal, not sixtyfold or thirtyfold. It doesn't matter if you have one small little thing to use, work it to its full potential. It doesn't matter where you have come from, at what state the economy is in, or in what condition is your church, your job, or your family. It is of no consequence who supports you or who doesn't support you. God has commanded His blessing over you because you have fully surrendered it all to Him. Therefore, nothing can hinder the seed of your gift from becoming the hundredfold abundance so that its fruit continues to bless you and your children's children for generations to come.

In the next chapter, I want to continue this process into abundance by finding the right partners and building a growing momentum with all God has entrusted to you.

QUESTIONS TO PONDER

1. What idea or product do you have that you can use as seed to begin a small step forward to see it increase?

_____

_____

_____

_____

2. Let's explore "What is in your hand?" List what you presently possess that could be used as a resource. What are some ideas to produce this into a tangible and profitable product?

_____

_____

_____

_____

3. List the fears you wrestle with that usually suggest you don't have much to give, you have no worthwhile abilities, and therefore, you've got nothing to increase. With God's ability,

what step could you take to overcome these fears allowing God to breathe upon your efforts?

_____

_____

_____

_____

4. As you read the story of my wife, Heather, is there a particular issue on your heart or a people group that came to mind that you really want to help? What are the first steps you could take to move toward that dream of yours?

_____

_____

_____

_____

_____

Eleven

GOOD RELATIONSHIPS ARE INVALUABLE

Getting to a new place of breakthrough in your life is not just dependent upon what you have, but it's also about who you know. The people you are connected with can often help you break free of a poverty mindset by brainstorming ways to multiply the seed of your talents, resources, and ideas right into your place of destiny.

It is important to take stock of relationships beyond your immediate family and those that you interact with on a regular basis and analyze how they are influencing your life choices. When you engage with people who are not going after anything bigger than they are, and who settle for living in a place of lack with a mindset that says, "Nothing good ever comes my way" . . . "Nobody cares about me" . . . or "I never seem to get a break!", you will always feel powerless to step into your destiny or dreams. If you truly want to see breakthrough in your life, you have to break completely away from all thinking patterns and sometimes even relationships that hinder your progress. Moving into a place of destiny may require a location change, finding new friends who dream big impossible dreams, and possibly joining a new community of friends who engage with the world with the broader goals of the Kingdom. If the place you're at has caused you to settle for less, you'll never break out or break through into the greater. If you want to be a giant killer, hang out with giant killers!

Nurturing the Good Seed

David was just that kind of young man—a mighty giant killer—and then he raised up an army of mighty men who also killed giants and later went on to achieve even greater exploits than his own. These men rallied around him because they saw something in him they desired in themselves. But take a look at the condition of David's men when they first joined him.

> *All those who were in distress or in debt or discontented gathered around him, and he became their commander. About four hundred men were with him.*
>
> 1 Samuel 22:2

Initially, these were not mighty men; they all had issues. The seed of the mighty was already within them, but it needed nurturing. As they followed David around for a few years while he escaped to the desert and hid from Saul's unrelenting pursuits, his men eventually transformed into "mighty men."[11] They became warriors who did some outrageously courageous military achievements as they safeguarded their leader, defended farmlands, killed scores of enemies singlehandedly, slayed giants, secured Israel from their marauding enemies, and gave their lives sacrificially for a greater cause than their own livelihood.

The Greater Cause

Great men possessing internal wealth view life larger than themselves. Their goal of gaining momentum is not to simply prosper themselves, but to aid in the prosperity of others toward the greater cause. Sometimes we come to a point in our lives in which we recognize that to go to the next level of development, we need a change of surroundings. Now, this can happen one of two ways. God can upgrade our relationships outside of our immediate family in our present environment, or He can move us to another location into a different church, a job change, or a new interest group of like-minded friends. If you want to become a giant killer, you are going to have to find others who think like you!

For me to step into becoming a resource, I needed to hang around people who were thinking way outside my box. Over the years, Heather and I have had the privilege and honor of many powerfully prophetic men and women speak into our lives. As I shared before, changing our physical residence allowed us to pursue our dreams of impacting the nations and training people to operate fully in the supernatural.

Transitions Develop New Kingdom Tracks

The challenge in moving to a new location came in ways we were not expecting or prepared for. When it was time to leave, we didn't experience problems with those who had challenged us the most, but with those with whom we had been the closest. That was a real surprise. These were good friends with whom we had fought Kingdom battles, and yet they resisted the new direction where God was sending us. They were about to lose their senior leader and they did not comprehend how that could possibly be God. But we knew it was God's way of helping us step into a greater expression of our call as much as it was His way of helping them step into destinies that, had we stayed, would not have been possible to live out. We had all developed relationships that had become very comfortable but that would have undoubtedly crippled us in our God-destinies had we not pursued His specific leading.

One of the benefits we experienced along our journey was the privilege to interact more often with those we considered giant killers. Previously we would only see them at a conference here and there or at a church where they were speaking, but it was entirely different to rub shoulders with them on a regular ongoing basis. I am so thankful for those that I have had the privilege to be with in recent years. These relationships provided the nurturing environment where I was able to mature into a much more secure leader than I would have been had I not made the painful transition and moved forward.

Good Friends Help Forge New Paths

I'm so thankful to God for the many friends and deep relationships He has given me through the years. My friend, Dan McCollam, has been an especially powerful influence and friend in my life. He has taught me so many things, and for that, I will be forever grateful. His friendship has provided wisdom, counsel, love, and a safe place to process and develop because he believed in me and in what God was doing in and through me. Dan provided numerous ways to define and refine my products as well as open doors for me to minister and teach. Good friendships like his are invaluable.

In order to go to the next level in your life, you need to assess what that level is. To do this, ask yourself some questions. As you do, give it some good thought and write down anything significant that comes to mind to process.

- What is it you are going after?

- What are your dreams?

- What are the resources you hope to develop one day?

- Do you have a desire and skills for business? For the financial marketplace?

- Do you have a passion to influence your nation? Your state? Your city? Other nations? Specific people groups?

- Do you have a heart to work with orphans, widows, the abused, underprivileged and oppressed?

- Do you have a desire to write and record songs, write books, or become an artist one day?

- Do you have a passion to transform cities by touching the lives of children, the homeless, and others sidelined in our society?

- Do you want to develop the skills and ideas you have inside to break poverty off your own life so you can make a significant difference in the world?

These are some of the questions I have asked myself as I considered the next step to where I wanted to be in my life. Going after any of these goals will require the wisdom of those who are experienced and skilled in their field. The knowledge your friends have gained in these arenas will be an invaluable help to you.

Some people desire to do something great, but they have relational issues that need to be worked out. For instance, an inability to get along with their leaders inhibits their progress. They have not learned to trust their leaders and therefore are unteachable. This may be because they have been hurt in the past by leaders and have not yet resolved this issue. Unless it is healed, this same issue will continue to hinder them from fully realizing their destiny. Healthy relationships—especially with your leaders—is the most constructive environment for all the demands toward your destiny. Maintaining good relationships with the leaders in your life assures you of a strong and powerful support team for everything God has yet ahead of you.

For me to get from Willits to Vacaville, I needed to receive favorable feedback from my mentors. These were ones who had been helping shape my life and refine the gifts and callings that I was stewarding at the time. Dano and I, along with our wives, had met early on, and Dano asked me the one question that changed everything: "If time or money weren't an issue, what would you be doing?" Through processing this question of his, I uncovered my passion to travel to the nations and develop supernatural schools that transform people to impact their world. When Dano heard what was in my heart, he and David Crone invited our family to move to Vacaville. They had thought about me coming to help but didn't know I carried a passion to develop supernatural schools. When they found out I wanted to do this, they called my main mentor at the time, Kris Vallotton, and in talking with him, agreed that this would be a good step for Heather and I; they both felt we were ready for it. Promotion comes from the Lord, but God's way also includes promotion through man. I think the partnership of God and man's agreement is necessary for any increase in our lives.

Prove You are Trustworthy

As we know, Jesus also grew in favor with God and man. Some are rich in their relationship with God and spiritual matters but haven't built the kind of trust needed to allow mentors and friends to influence their lives. It's often a trust factor. Kris Vallotton told us early on that when we had reached the point where we were fulfilling what God had put in our hearts to do, some would think it was the anointing or other things that got us there. "But," he instructed, "it really is the fact that you allowed every area of your lives to be spoken into that elevated you." And that is what we sought to do.

As time went on, my first door into a particular nation came through Kris and Dano's mutual agreement. I didn't know this, but both of them were testing me out to see how I would do. Kris traveled to that country when I had finished my time there and noticed that the atmosphere had advanced to a much higher level of breakthrough than the previous year when he had been there. He told me, "I knew breakthrough occurred because you had been here ministering before I arrived. It was clearly evident in the atmosphere, and because of that, I will send you more opportunities." From that time on, Kris provided more open doors for me. Now some of you reading this may think, *Well I don't have access to a well-known person to get to the next level.* But know this, God will always give you what you need to succeed in life that will bring you to the next level where He wants you to be. He is always after your full maturity and positions you for its most effective process.

Nurture Your Divine Relationships

You have to take inventory of your relationships. Many times, we try to pick and choose or even push into relationships that were never meant for us. Whereas divine connections are just that—God-ordained. Sometimes they do demand an active pursuit on our part, and may even require sacrifice. I remember in the early years of revival we were so hungry for God that we would fly across the country just to be in meetings where He was showing up. We waited in lines for hours and hours and jumped at every chance to be prayed for by those who carried the anointing we desired.

Sometimes relationships of significance require hard work and proactive personal investment. For instance, if you want to become a successful businessman, you need to identify those who are successful in that specific business type. If you cannot locate any where you are, then look online where you can glean from those from whom you want to learn. Find out if there are books about that business, look for CDs, podcasts, or YouTube videos, locate any conferences, seminars or schools to attend, etc. Search for any and all resource material and tools that will help take your skills to the next level.

There are many ways to gain favor and influence to become an influencer. One businessman I know had a desire to be an influencer in the church world but lacked trust in his own pastor. I shared with him: "The key to doors opening up for you in the church world includes building a bridge between you and your pastor. I want to suggest that you begin by viewing your pastor in a positive light, as someone who is *for* you instead of someone who is against you." God purposefully puts doorkeepers in our paths with whom we have to pass a test in order to be entrusted with greater authority and influence. We simply must mature in our interpersonal relationships, especially with those God has put over us. We have to be mindful of the fact that they may not be fully cognizant of our personal needs and desires, and for that we must extend much grace to them, not criticism.

Over the next couple of years, this businessman went through the difficult process of changing the way he viewed his leader by building a bridge of trust with him as I recommended, and he found practical ways to use his own gifts and skills that sought to build up the Body instead of tearing it down through criticism. As a result, his pastor began to trust him more, and doors are being opened where he is able to fulfill his dream of being an influence to the church at large.

Sometimes it is only the first door a leader opens up to us. But if you are unable to get even the first door open, you won't be able to get to the second. The first may not be the biggest opportunity you step into, but it may be the most important door to step through at that time. How you steward the growing favor you are given—no matter how difficult or seemingly insignificant it may be—determines if and when you receive more favor.

As I have developed into becoming a resource to the Body of Christ, I have made many mistakes. I am a learner by nature, a disciple, and love to grow and increase. When I stepped into the arena of being part of a team of other giant killers, it put me on a much greater path of learning. Mistakes that I make in this arena have greater impact, and therefore, require greater wisdom to avoid, as much as is possible. Sometimes, however, we have to make a mistake to learn from it in order to go to the next level. But if we posture ourselves in a teachable, humble position, alongside of our good friends, we will find that mistakes can become stepping-stones to greater success.

Successful Relational Connections

Several years ago, at a church I had been invited to work with, I immediately saw something in the spirit that was coming between several of the leaders on the team. I spoke publicly into that issue at the evening meeting because I felt it over the congregation as well. In doing so, one of those two leaders took it personally. They thought I was using the pulpit to speak to something wrong in them.

One of my mentors had opened the door for me to speak at this particular church, and so it was a brand new relationship for me, which made this situation doubly awkward. After the service, I talked this through with the main leader and he told me to speak to his other leader about what I saw in him. I wasn't sure if I should do this since I didn't even have much of a relationship with him. I called one of my mentors and asked him what he thought I should do. "Go for it, Keith," he told me. "Helping the senior leader deal with in-house issues is always a benefit."

I took his advice and spoke to the leader directly. Well, it didn't go over very well. In fact, it sent both of the leaders into a bit of a tailspin, and they spoke with several of the leaders above them about what I had shared. But other leaders had also been seeing the same issue for a long time; they just hadn't addressed it. So when I showed up and hit it head on, the whole issue was brought out into the bright light where it had to be dealt with.

The situation got messier before it got healthier. It took a year and a half of working really hard at building relationally into both of those team members to gain their confidence. After all the time I invested, they both came to trust me and have allowed me, along with a few others, to be a part of the process of leading them through successfully.

Did I handle the situation correctly from the start? Probably not. Should I have spoken to what I saw publicly? I don't believe so. Should I have spoken with that leader in whom I saw the issue but with whom I had very little relationally? In hindsight, no. I repented of making things so messy. I worked at trying to learn from that situation by making myself vulnerable to those leaders' critique as well as my own leadership team at home. Those situations, however uncomfortable, can become doorways into greater influence if we seek to handle them correctly. Even if we make a bit of a mess, we can grow because of it if we remain humble and teachable. God will pull us through and raise us up out of them. We're going for successful relational connections at every opportunity, and as we do that, God will use that door to open up other doors of influence for us.

Expect Relational Challenges and Upgrades

In another country, I walked through a door of favor that God Himself opened up for me. This church has been one of the most influential churches in the Christian world and one that I had greatly admired since my childhood. I was invited to speak in this church for several meetings by another relationship of that same nation that I had been stewarding and building up trust for several years. This person spoke to his pastor and told him that he should have me speak in his church to bring my message of joy.

When I first met the pastor of this church, I sort of cringed. His mannerisms reminded me of the old way of serving God that I had come out of, and he felt a bit cold and religiously stiff. Our first meal together was rather awkward, to say the least, as he quizzed me about my biblical stand on this issue and that issue. We seemed to be on opposite ends of each one of them. I was sitting there thinking to myself, *Debating theological issues is not what I wanted to do tonight! I sure don't want to end this conversation on such a negative note . . . Why are we arguing about what we believe? It's leading us nowhere . . . How do I get out of this? Lord, help! . . .* In my estimation, dinner with the lead pastor and the first meeting that night did not go too well. When I was finally finished for the evening, I returned to my hotel room, plopped down, and flipped on a James Bond movie. Sometimes, after a stressful situation, watching something on TV helps me unwind. In the movie, a couple phrases caught my attention, and I knew the Lord was speaking to me.

"M", who is Bond's boss, was ridiculing him for making a big mess over some situations in which he was involved. She told James Bond something like, "I knew this promotion was too soon for you . . . you're just killing people right and left and not going along with the plan."

Bond replied back rather arrogantly, "Well, you'll be through with me soon enough . . . 007s are short-lived."

Immediately I heard the Lord say to me: "Keith, I have promoted you by giving you this place of influence to speak into. You need to realize that this pastor is your brother, and therefore, you need to love him as such." That arrow went straight in and had its transforming effect on my heart.

The next day when I met the same pastor again for lunch, I approached him very differently. I began to ask him some questions, but with a heart determined to learn.

"Pastor, I'd really love to hear what it was like being a part of one of the most influential churches of our time. What were some of the things you learned from your many years of being on staff of that church?" Immediately his guard came down, his face softened, and his stiff religious demeanor completely changed. He began to share with me valuable lessons he had learned over the years. As he did, the Lord unveiled a prophetic word for me to release over him. Here we were at this very posh restaurant eating a gourmet meal, but that word so impacted him, he told me, "Oh . . . how I wish I could have recorded that."

Then I heard the Lord say to me, "Prophesy it again!" So I opened my mouth and began to prophesy it all once again, but this time, he had his phone ready to record it.

When I finished, he played it back to hear it all once again, word for word. "Is this what the Lord says about me?" He asked in wonder and amazement. "Am I really going to do this?" The pastor was blown away and completely changed in that moment. Returning back to the church offices, he went around letting people hear the recording of what I had prophesied over him.

That night at the meeting, the people were eagerly expectant and impacted at a much higher level. I released my message on joy, and then in partnership with that tangible joy present in the sanctuary, I prayed for many who needed physical healing. We had several significant miracles that night along with the release of laughter and praise. When I turned the meeting back over to the pastor, he was undone. He followed up my message with his own message to his people: "Friends, we have been too serious for too long! The whole church really needs this message!" For decades, his church was well known for their strong values on prayer and modeled this standard for the church around the world to follow. He told his congregation that he would be changing their all-night weekly prayer meetings to joy-filled healing services! He wasn't certain how it would all go but he was willing to step out in faith to move forward in it. Joy had become the new model of prayer and healing from here on.

A Friend Who Opens Doors

Later on, I learned that whatever this pastor modeled in his church was then modeled in other churches within his movement, including one of the largest churches in the world. The door into that nation was through my friend, Dano. Because he opened that door for me, this particular pastor was forever impacted. That's the way it works. When you are faithful with one door, God gives you another that can lead to another and another . . . and at some point, one of those doors will bring a significant and enduring breakthrough. You don't have to worry about all the doors that need to open. You just need to be faithful to the one relationship that God has given you to learn from and be faithful in that relationship.

Take a review of your present relationships and perhaps make a list of them. Is there someone that you have access to who can help you get to where you need to go? Is there a person in your life that you have perhaps overlooked who actually offered to help you, but you were looking for help elsewhere? Sometimes we miss the door because we are looking in a very different direction. But it might be that we need to step back and consider what is the initial step that we should take. Remember, God always gives us the next step that is directly connected to the dream in our heart if we will pay attention to it.

I asked my dad some years ago about how the doors opened for him to step into other churches to pastor. He said the door always opened through someone he already knew. A relationship that was built from the past season is a door that often helps open the very next door.

Joseph's faithfulness in prison was the key to opening the door to his influence in the palace.

> *Then the chief cupbearer said to Pharaoh, "Today I am reminded of my shortcomings. Pharaoh was once angry with his servants, and he imprisoned me and the chief baker in the house of the captain of the guard. Each of us had a dream the same night, and each dream had a meaning of its own. Now a young Hebrew was there with us, a servant of the captain of the guard. We told him our dreams, and he interpreted them for us, giving each man the interpretation of his dream. And things turned out exactly as he interpreted them to us: I was restored to my position, and the other man was impaled." So, Pharaoh sent for Joseph, and he was quickly brought from the dungeon. When he had shaved and changed his clothes, he came before Pharaoh.*
>
> Genesis 41:9 -15

Joseph continued to rise up and be a leader in whatever environment he found himself. The situation didn't matter, because God's favor and influence works wherever we are. It was Joseph's gifts in leadership, wisdom, and prophetic intuition that caused him to be recommended to the king, which eventually promoted him to the high level from where he was destined to rule.

The faithfulness with using your gifts in the place where God has currently assigned you is the key to doors opening to greater realms of influence. We should never seek a promotion. Instead, we should use our gifts and talents to the best of our abilities so that we can grow to handle the favor that promotion brings. When we allow people who are accessible to develop our gifts and skills, then we will have developed into ones who are trustworthy and can handle greater levels of increased influence and wealth without crumbling.

In the next chapter, I want to explore who we need to partner with in order to see greater increase in our lives.

QUESTIONS TO PONDER

1. Who are the people in your world who can help move you forward in your dreams or pursuit of increased resources or finances? Take some time to identify them.

_____

_____

_____

2. Have you done a good job of building trust with these individuals or have you had a history of burning relational bridges? If so, what are some practical adjustments you can make to change this pattern?

_____

_____

_____

_____

3. Are there any relational messes you need to mend before God can entrust you with more influence? Are there people from whom you need to ask forgiveness for your past actions? If need be, how could you make restitution in order to move forward?

_____

_____

4. Do you have anyone who has offered to mentor you but you have resisted? What could you learn from them? List these. Considering the place where you are at present, take some time to consider how a mentor could help move you forward.

_____

_____

_____

_____

_____

_____

_____

_____

Twelve

PARTNER FOR INCREASE

*L*earning to glean from others is key to increasing what you already have. Why go through the long and difficult years of acquiring something that someone else already knows how to do? Why not posture yourself with a teachable attitude and receive the blessing of inheritance? Just as learning to glean from others is important, learning to partner with others is just as important.

It can be extremely helpful to find the missing piece you really need in someone else. Many these days have an independent mindset. They think, *I must figure out how to get what I need by myself.* But in reality, if you want something, you have to discover the people with whom you need to partner to achieve your desired goal. Sometimes it is not about you doing more and more, but about you coming into divine relational connections. Many great people come into a place of high level influence because they had someone who partnered with them, which empowered them to accomplish even greater things than they would have on their own. This is an important Kingdom principle to take to heart and apply to your life.

Development and Administration

I learned this key when I was pastoring. At our church in Willits, I had invested about seven years in leading our worship team. During that time, I learned how to pastor all the elements of worship and worked closely with the team members. We had a solid band who was passionate for Jesus and loved His presence. We regularly held extended worship times to soak in His presence and often continued the worship long after the service, sometimes until the very last person left! We had a high value for worshiping God!

But it wasn't until Rick McCoy came along that our worship bands multiplied and matured to a whole new level. When I led worship, it was marked by a spontaneous prophetic flow, which I love. Rick, on the other hand, was great at developing consistency in people and putting together a worship set (a sequence of songs sung during worship). With the transfer of leadership to Rick, he was able to pastor the worship team with even greater excellence so that he raised up four worship leaders as well as a solid selection of musicians, allowing for a regular rotation. While I was great at inspiring a spontaneous flow, Rick's strength was in the details of development and administration. We were a strong team.

At this time we also took on a building project to remodel our traditional-style church into a more modern feel. I was good at communicating vision and making the necessary big decisions that paved the way for change, while Rick was the one who administered the nitty-gritty details of the building project. He took care of all the practical hands-on work, the day-to-day organization, coordinating with the construction crews, planning the lighting and sound system, etc. He was ultimately able to bring what we first envisioned right on through to its full completion. He had the gifting to take what I dreamed and turn it into a reality. I have seen this again and again with well-matched partners. The fact is, you can only go so far by yourself, but paired with someone alongside of you who has a broader, full-picture perspective, you can do so much more.

Armor Bearers

In the Bible, Jonathan had an amazing armor bearer who stood right alongside of him. Without him, he would not have had the synergy needed to take out the enemy when they taunted Israel.

> *Jonathan said to his young armor-bearer, "Come, and let's go over to the outpost of those uncircumcised men. Perhaps the LORD will act in our behalf. Nothing can hinder the LORD from saving, whether by many or by few."*
>
> *"Do all that you have in mind," his armor-bearer said. "Go ahead; I am with you heart and soul."*
>
> 1 Samuel 14:6-7

The agreement with another like-minded person was all that was needed to propel Jonathan forward into victory. Jesus understood this principle, and so He sent out His disciples in pairs to expand the Kingdom.

After this the Lord appointed seventy-two others and sent them two by two ahead of him to every town and place where he was about to go.

Luke 10:1

My brother, Paul, was my armor bearer for many years while I was pastoring. Sometimes we would go on a prayer walk to the top of a mountain, and other times we'd walk and pray through local areas. He always had my back and knew how to protect me through intercession as well as how to deal with the enemy while we were on assignments. He also served as my armor bearer in church meetings, keeping an eye out to protect my space as I ministered so that nothing and no one would hinder what God intended to do. That protection helped create a resting place for me in the spirit so I didn't have to be vigilant in my environment, but could rest knowing someone was on duty.

Watchmen

The Lord brought another supportive armor bearer into my life, Tom Parsons. He carries an amazing intercessory seer gift that allows him to stand guard in the heavenlies, so that whether he is with me or not, his watchman anointing becomes a shield of protection over me as I am flowing in ministry partnership with the Spirit. Countless times he has felt or seen something significant in that watchman place of the Spirit and shared it with me. Those insights gave me the much-needed encouragement and breakthrough strategy to address it head-on and release that specific thing God showed him. At times, Tom has sent me an email with words of knowledge for healing, even though he may be several thousand miles away from where I was ministering. As I released his words of knowledge in the meeting place where I was, the heavens opened up for healing and many were healed because I partnered with his insights.

There have been many times he has seen the plans of the enemy, pointed them out to me, and then dealt with it in one swift prayer. As he did, I felt an instant change within me, and my spirit experienced a renewed sense of freedom—prior to the breakthrough needed where I would be engaged in a particularly difficult spiritual climate. Having partners and armor bearers like my brother, Paul, and my friend, Tom, have made my ministry so much easier, and I honestly don't know what I would do without their support.

I have noticed when I go places with such friends who have specific spiritual giftings, the atmosphere opens up easier in the spirit than when I do the meeting alone. When I took Rick McCoy with me to Korea for ten days of ministry, for instance, I had a significant increase in miracles and healings because he consistently asked the Lord for words of knowledge. I can flow in words of knowledge too, but it was a tremendous advantage having someone else accessing that gift ahead of time. When Rick released those words, I could easily step into that grace and help facilitate a greater release of breakthrough than I could on my own. I love the power of team and the multiplication of breakthroughs you get when you partner with others.

I recommend that you look for like-minded people who will work alongside of you as armor bearers and watchmen. God is sending them your way.

Develop the Weaker Areas

The key is to do what you do best and find others who excel in areas that are not your strengths. There are times to really stretch and work the undeveloped areas of our lives and God will provide seasons to do just that. Sometimes He has us in a season of assignment—a very specific place—to develop skills that will help us later in the season of dreaming. In that specific season of assignment, we are often developing areas of weakness, character, perseverance, and so on, that will carry us through to the next season.

In my years of pastoring, I never wanted to be a pastor because the relational part scared me. I had grown up seeing people hurt one another, and I didn't want to experience that. So I figured I should instead be a fiery evangelist who goes from church to church saying, "Stop it!" Instead, God told me that I needed to pastor a church and learn to develop a relational culture through *love*. That season was ten years of developing the very area that was my weakest. I had a lot of great help from within the church and mentors from elsewhere. That was a necessary season for me in learning skills I wasn't naturally talented or gifted in. On the other hand, I have noticed that when entering a season of dreaming, it often requires that you learn new skills while still functioning within your current skills and gifts. That means you have to find others to make up what you lack.

Look for Strengths in Others

If you are a great starter in projects and can easily think up lots and lots of ideas, then it would be good to find someone who is a great finisher and can put legs to your ideas. If you are a great finisher, then find that person who is a skilled organizer and who can easily see the initial steps necessary to begin the process of momentum towards the finish line. Like my friend, Rick, their anointing is in the structure and minute details. Maybe you have a passion for being part of developing something from the ground up. Recognizing whether you are the initiator of that project or the finisher will be the difference between success and failure. Finding the partners who hold the same heart and passion for the project but who also have a well-developed and unique skill set to contribute will be key to a final outcome that carries the weight of His anointing.

For those of us who grew up in the church world, we were taught a strong ethic of serving, often helping out whatever was needed. Serving is a great skill to learn; but if you are to gain momentum towards your destiny, you have to learn to hone in on an area of your greatest passion instead of expending your energies on the drudgery tasks. There is no synergy or momentum when you are laboring where you're not gifted or excited about it. Instead, the work will lack momentum and just be tedious. It's so exhausting to do this kind of work when your heart is not in it, where you find you have to pep-talk yourself into it finishing the task at hand. Unfortunately, this is how many people regularly manage their lives. They stay put in laborious departments of their job, church roles, or ministry activities but have little or no passion for it. They do it because it needs to be done or they feel compelled. Mind you, there will always be jobs that we are obliged to do and that we may not be great at, but the primary use of our energies should be in the areas of our expertise, experience, and desire. When we focus on those things—the passion of our heart—we find our sweet spot, and our whole life flourishes. It energizes us! Attend fully to these activities on your heart, and then look for partners who have the missing pieces and strengths you need to complete it.

Work through the Differences

Paul and Barnabas seemed to be a partner match from Heaven. Paul was the main speaker and Barnabas the encourager. They both taught, but Barnabas had this ability to work with those who had some issues until they were brought to a place of usefulness. The challenge in working with someone different than you is that you think and process life differently. We often stumble over someone else's differences in gifting instead of appreciating that it is actually a unique blessing. I am not pastoral in gifting, but I have learned to be pastoral in heart, because I have gleaned from others who carry that genuine gift. I have also learned to appreciate the pastorally-gifted people in my life because they help me maintain a healthy perspective on people where my prophetic gifting tends to focus on the areas that need growth.

Unfortunately, Paul and Barnabas had such a sharp dispute over their differences about a specific person on their team, they severed their ministry partnership.

> *Barnabas wanted to take John, also called Mark, with them, but Paul did not think it wise to take him, because he had deserted them in Pamphylia and had not continued with them in the work. They had such a sharp disagreement that they parted company, Barnabas took Mark and sailed for Cyprus, but Paul chose Silas and left . . .*
>
> Acts 15:37-40

What a sad separation this was. Later, we see that Paul came to see the same value in John Mark that Barnabas had seen and he seeks him out once again.

> *Get Mark and bring him with you, because he is helpful to me in my ministry.*
>
> 2 Timothy 4:11b

Even though Paul chose Silas to be his new ministry partner instead, it just wasn't the same synergetic teamwork as he had with Barnabas. I find this a good lesson of working through differences within our teams and partners.

Honor and Diversity

The challenge of having varying gift mixes around us is that each one thinks and acts differently. That is certainly a blessing, but it stretches us as well. It is much easier to gather people to us who are similar, those who exhibit similar thinking patterns and opinions. It creates fewer waves in staff meetings, that's for sure, but quite honestly, less gets done. I have come to really appreciate the unique distinctions in others. The key to holding this together is a culture where we develop and nurture honor. About this, Bill Johnson says:

> Honor is the ability to value who someone is without stumbling over who they are not.

In short, what they are, we so desperately need; what they are not, others bring to the table to complete the puzzle. The beauty of the puzzle is found in the ability to identify which pieces need to go where to complete the picture of what God wants to do in and through you. The amazing thing about it is that as God carefully selects those individuals to help complete what you need, you will in turn bring some level of completion to what they need as well. If the Body is functioning properly in this way, every piece will be working in that perfect place of grace that fulfills their personal dream but also completes and serves each other's need. I Corinthians 12 says it so well:

> *Even so the body is not made up of one part but of many. Now if the foot should say, "Because I am not a hand, I do not belong to the body," it would not for that reason stop being part of the body. And if the ear should say, "Because I am not an eye, I do not belong to the body," it would not for that reason stop being part of the body.*

If the whole body were an eye, where would the sense of hearing be? If the whole body were an ear, where would the sense of smell be? But in fact God has placed the parts in the body, every one of them, just as he wanted them to be. If they were all one part, where would the body be? As it is, there are many parts, but one body. The eye cannot say to the hand, "I don't need you!" And the head cannot say to the feet, "I don't need you!" On the contrary, those parts of the body that seem to be weaker are indispensable, and the parts that we think are less honorable we treat with special honor. And the parts that are unpresentable are treated with special modesty, while our presentable parts need no special treatment. But God has put the body together, giving greater honor to the parts that lacked it, so that there should be no division in the body, but that its parts should have equal concern for each other. If one part suffers, every part suffers with it; if one part is honored, every part rejoices with it. Now you are the body of Christ, and each one of you is a part of it.

vs 14-27

This is the key to teamwork and to stepping into a place of multiplication in your life, your business, dream, or ministry. Learn to value the differences in others; search out what is the glorious inheritance in the saints all around you and utilize them. What are the hidden treasures of wealth, gifting, and wisdom that are in the people you know? It is a fun exploration! Learn to value and appreciate those differences and see them as treasures to seek out. Find people who carry something complimentary to your needs and develop a partnership with them. One can put one thousand to flight and two ten thousand. What a great increase when you find those significant partnerships.

In the final chapter, I want to discuss developing the mindset that the wealthy exhibit naturally, one that sees numerous possibilities and multiple streams of income, and accesses them to create sustainability and ultimately, a legacy.

QUESTIONS TO PONDER

1. What kind of a different gifting do you need to help advance the dreams of your heart? Do you know a person that carries that? Is it someone with whom you could build a partnership? What is the first step towards developing that relationship?

_____

_____

_____

_____

2. Have you had a partner with whom you worked closely in ministry, work, or life? What were the strengths and weaknesses of that relationship? Did the relationship continue? Explain. Are there areas you need to grow in to be able to work well in a future partnership to achieve a Kingdom goal?

_____

_____

_____

_____

_____

_____

Thirteen

STREAMS OF INCOME

I believe the Lord wants each one of us continually blessed and financially secure. There is no lack in Heaven, so the goal is to eliminate lack wherever it is found. Lack is a mindset that manifests in the physical realm and is evidenced by an absence of love, sustainable income, or acts of generous compassion. The goal should rather be abundance in every area of your life so that generosity flows outward from a heart of love and compassion through your spiritual gifts, skills, finances, time and resources.

You can have an abundance in one area, but lack in others. For instance, one may have an abundance in healing anointing because he has accessed the abundance of Heaven to bring it to those in need. It flows easily and freely through him and he sees many healings because of a revelation of what is available and accessible to him in that area. But he seems to really struggle with finances and suffers lack all the time. He just doesn't see financial abundance; the provision he needs day to day is slow to come, and when it finally does come, it often is barely enough. I know what that's like. I remember a time when I was praying for someone to be healed, and right after they were healed, my mind wandered back to my ongoing financial concerns. There I was, worrying about how I was going to get my bills paid. The Lord spoke to me clearly and said, "Where did I go, Keith? A moment ago, I was present for healing. I'm still here . . . I also care about your finances." You see, we can be rich in heavenly resources in one area and depleted in another. But ultimately, God's desire is that we receive a revelation of what is available for that impoverished area where we lack and choose to live in the wealth of Heaven's abundant resources.

> *For whoever has will be given more, and they will have an abundance. Whoever does not have, even what they have will be taken from them.*
>
> Matthew 25:29

God has determined that you will not suffer lack or be in poverty, but that you will prosper in every area of your life. Here's what Paul says in 2 Corinthians 9:

> *Now he who supplies seed to the sower and bread for food will also supply and increase your store of seed and will enlarge the harvest of your righteousness. You will be enriched in every way so that you can be generous on every occasion, and through us your generosity will result in thanksgiving to God.*
>
> vs 10-11

I love these passages that demonstrate God's heart. He has more than enough for each one of us and gives us seed to sow to guarantee that we will have an abundant harvest. In fact, according to these verses, we will be rich in every way so that we can be generous on every occasion! There's absolutely no lack there! Some people have a problem with the word "rich" because they may think it refers to a socio-economic class they are unfamiliar with. But this is referring to a rich mindset. For instance, you can be poor in finances but rich in heart. The poor widow who gave two mites was considered rich, in that, by comparison to those who gave a little bit out of their wealth, she gave all she had—her last dime, so to speak. She exemplified the most generous giver out of them all because she had no surplus to pool from, but her generous heart demanded that she give to God, so she gave it all! Generosity and riches are in proportion to what God has given us. When we are faithful to give, work, and sow what we've been given, then we will experience an abundant provision for all that is in our heart to do.

God's abundance will reflect in every area of our lives *to the degree we allow Him.* We can have all we need, sufficient to live, and more than enough with which to be generous and share with others. As we saw in Matthew 25:29, those who have, *more* will be given to them so that they will have *an abundance.*

I like what Kris Vallotton says about wealth and abundance:

> The question is not about whether you have possessions, money or things; but rather, does it have you?

God's blessings are in all He gives, including our riches and possessions. They are also tools whereby we can prosper and do well so we can live without worry about where our next meal will come from. We also have the great privilege of contributing to increase His Kingdom with the profits we gain. Pursuing the things God has put on our heart is the true test of the heart attachments to our wealth and possessions and an indication that you are rightly appropriating what you have in order to advance your resources.

Consider what Jesus said to those who did not properly invest the riches they were given.

> *Then the man who had received the one bag of gold came. "Master," he said, "I knew that you are a hard man, harvesting where you have not sown and gathering where you have not scattered seed. So I was afraid and went out and hid your gold in the ground. See, here is what belongs to you."*
>
> *His master replied, "You wicked, lazy servant! So you knew that I harvest where I have not sown and gather where I have not scattered seed? Well then, you should have put my money on deposit with the bankers, so that when I returned I would have received it back with interest."*
>
> Matthew 25:24-27

We are held accountable for all we have been given to not just guard it, but increase it!

A Little Seed Becomes an Orchard

Each one of us has been given a portion of money or an ability to make money. That money or ability to make money is considered a talent, and some have been given more than one talent. In this parable, one person was given five, another ten, and this particular man was given a single talent to work with. Whatever you have been given is sufficient for what you need. Sometimes we are gripped with fear that we will lack because we only have one small thing to use. But if you have one talent, a job, or an ability to make money, then the advantage for you will be to focus on that single area exclusively and invest all your time and energy into it. Get really good at it—be an expert in that field. Some people became wealthy doing just one thing well. The whole Facebook phenomenon is a good example. One simple idea of a young man to connect college students through the Internet turned into an incredible financial stream that made him a billionaire. Likewise, God has given you a good seed to plant, at least in one area. Find out what that is, plant it, nurture it—focus on it!—until it becomes an orchard, a stream of steady income for you to prosper. You may have two seeds, or five, or ten. Follow through in the same way with each one of them until they are productive and profitable.

There are several keys to developing streams of income that will bless you, sustain you, and ultimately open you up with opportunities to advance the Kingdom. But you first need a job. If you notice in this passage about the talents, the servant who was entrusted with this money did nothing with his job. He didn't work with it, he didn't go after it; he simply buried it, and it was like he sat there wondering what to do next. This inactivity and do-nothing attitude was labeled by the Lord, a "lazy servant". In my years of ministry, I have met a few of these who had a misunderstanding about what "living by faith" means. For some it means they have no plans to labor in a job; instead, they wait and hope that others will give them financial donations to live on. I believe this mindset can be a poverty, beggarly attitude and sometimes creates an unhealthy dependence upon people for their provision.

No matter our job in the Kingdom, finding creative ways to communicate our message and vision will also aid in contributing to our needs. It's God's provision and desire for us so that we prosper and do well. So it's good to ask ourselves: Are we relying on people for income or are we learning how to develop our own streams of income God has given us to develop?

"A Job" versus Your "Work"

So, what is a job? A job is different than work. A job provides a means to generate finances. As an example, I have a variety of "jobs" and each of these have become streams of income for me. I develop and release prophetic worship CDs, write books, offer consultation services for business people and prophets, develop sermons to offer as a product, I travel and teach, and I also oversee a number of ministries at the local church level. These are all sources of income for me, which allows me to do my "work".

My work is different than my job. "Work" is defined as the things you do that will affect eternity. My work is developing resources that bring people into Kingdom understanding to transform their world. Other work I do is preaching and teaching to encourage the Body, developing and encouraging leaders, and traveling to build up the Body in a variety of ways. It is a blessing that my job and my work are both in the same areas. The CDs, sermons, and books are all a part of my passions, and I enjoy developing them. They help others come into greater places in God and it gives me great joy to hear that these resources are a great blessing to those who receive them.

Sometimes a job and the work you are called to do differ, and that can create a challenge but can also be a blessing as well. I have many friends who work a salaried job but they are also actively engaged in their work for the Kingdom. This was true for Paul the Apostle. He was a tentmaker by trade, providing monetary sustenance for his personal needs. Paul was intent on setting an example of how to live working a job and also doing Kingdom work.

> *For you yourselves know how you ought to follow our example. We were not idle when we were with you, nor did we eat anyone's food without paying for it. On the contrary, we worked night and day, laboring and toiling so that we would not be a burden to any of you. We did this, not because we do not have the right to such help, but in order to offer ourselves as a model for you to imitate. For even when we were with you, we gave you this rule: "The one who is unwilling to work shall not eat."*

> 2 Thessalonians 3:7-10

Paul chose his tentmaking job instead of receiving income from his Kingdom work of preaching and teaching to model how each of us should contribute to society and not be a burden on any. The takeaway lesson here is that we are called to walk by faith, not solely live off the good graces of people, but rather, be a good steward of the talents, money, and skills God has given us.

It is nice when our job and work line up, but we have to learn not to devalue one over the other. God rebuked the lazy servant because he didn't increase the money he was given. Some people are simply working for money, but are not increasing their income. They are squeaking by in life and barely making it. To avoid this, ask God to help you learn to make money work for you.

Passive Income

Finding ways to generate sustainable income streams without you having to be actively engaged with it is a good way to make your money work for you. Take some time to consider what that could mean for you personally. Research your options and learn new skills as needed to set this in motion. The results are well worth it.

One way is to consider developing "passive income" so that a product pays you while you are free to go and do something else. You get to enjoy the fruit of it again and again. For example, whenever I write a book and make it available on Amazon.com, it generates income for me no matter where I am in the world. They do all the work for me: print, ship, and collect the sales from my product right from their website. No more work is required to receive a yield from that product; I'm reaping the benefits of the labor I put in to produce it, and it now contributes to my sustainable income.

There are countless online options available nowadays to tap into such income streams. You just have to find your niche where your gifts, skills, and creative ideas come together, plug in, and produce something from which others will profit and benefit.

Don't Look Back!

It's hard work to produce resources that make a good return, and along the way, you can encounter many frustrations during the long wait of its completion. During a season of unrelenting financial strain with no seeming way out, the temptation is to return back to where it seemed an easy place to make ends meet. The Israelites wanted to return to Egypt once they got into the harsh desert environment. Let's look at the passage that tells us why.

> *We remember the fish we ate in Egypt at no*
> *cost—also the cucumbers, melons, leeks, onions*
> *and garlic.*
>
> Numbers 11:5

They enjoyed the free food they received while working under forced labor, and they longed to go back. That word "freely" means without a cost; causeless; to cost nothing.[12] They thought entering into their Promised Land was going to be easy and fun, but then they found themselves in the dry, barren desert having to go out every day and gather their own food of manna and quail. Never mind that it was the food of angels direct from heaven; they longed instead for the food of Egypt that was free, effortless, and readily available. They were choosing to return to a meaningless, "causeless" existence, where they could be *fed* and taken care of. They resisted the desert life of laboring hard and expending their energies where God exercised them to be empowered and fully equipped to access their *own* resources once they crossed into their Promised Land. He intended they would never again be dependent slave laborers.

Promotion Brings Challenges

I remember when I first made my big move to Vacaville that God told me this was a part of my own promised land where I would see the dreams of my heart fulfilled. For some reason, I was under the impression that it was all going to be easy, just a bed of roses from here on. After all, this was my promised land! I had arrived! Back in Willits, I had already paid a high cost to bring the Kingdom and thought a good rest would be in order. Instead, I found myself having to work harder than ever before. I was put into one growth curve after another and elevated to higher and higher levels than ever before. The pressure was mounting, and I realized that this was not at *all* what I expected! I had begun the work I was called to do: traveling to foreign nations, developing schools of the supernatural, and even impacting the church on a wider scale. But the sacrifice, the daily struggles, the increased emotional strength needed, taking on new leadership skills, and the relational challenges of team cooperatives was not what I had in mind.

Work Hard!

However, if we are to expect an increase in what God has given us, if we are truly advancing toward our abundance, we must be willing to work hard for it, no matter the difficulties or personal cost. This is key to developing streams of income: have a mind to work hard! That's what it takes. As in the passage of the parable of the talents, the master understood that resource advancement was going to require a lot of hard work and not a misrepresented faith with false claims of easy, no-work provision. While God abundantly provides all we need, He expects our active participation to wisely invest our "talent" for a profitable return. Consider what Paul says regarding our "needs" and our working contribution towards that.

> *And my God will meet all your needs according to the riches of his glory in Christ Jesus.*
>
> Philippians 4:19

The word "needs"[13] has many definitions, and one definition of it in the Greek is "employment" or jobs. So it could read like this: "My God will meet[14] [or "supply" in KJV] all your **jobs** according to His riches in glory." It takes faith to believe God to provide good jobs that will generate income for us so we can do the Kingdom work He has called us to do. The seed that God gives us to sow at times includes jobs that we are required to work until we have a return, and from that return, we can sow it and see it begin to benefit and bless others. Sometimes we work in jobs that are difficult or may seem pointless because it is simply earning us income that pays our bills. That's okay. Such a job will generate a steady income that will help you develop your Kingdom work.

God's Benefits and Rewards

Jesus speaks about the eternal value of the work we do:

> *Do not work for food that spoils, but for food that endures to eternal life, which the Son of Man will give you. For on him God the Father has placed his seal of approval.*

John 6:2 7

What He is saying is, "It is okay to work for food, but don't let that be the main reason you are working." The work you should be doing includes bringing a greater expression of Heaven into the arenas you have been assigned and are passionate to transform. We are going to be called to account for the work we did on earth that was marked with eternity. Make sure you are producing resources that encourage the Body around the globe to be fired up with the passion of Heaven from an eternal perspective. Kingdom work does not have to be preaching, but all true work is advancing Heaven's agenda through your unique creative expression into whatever arena you have been assigned. Every arena is His, and that includes government, business and finance, recreation and sports, the arts, religion, family, cities and nations.

Some of us have a passion for transforming and empowering people through a variety of means: some through social work, others through bringing the message of salvation to those in the workplace, some through varied creative channels, etc. All of these works are viable expressions that will stand the test of eternity as we seek to make our heavenly Father's Kingdom famous. If we are desirous to make Him famous through the work we do, then whether we are a janitor or preach the gospel to the masses, our reward is sure.

As you are faithful with what you have been given—one talent, five, or ten—you will receive your rewards, the abundance of Heaven promised to us:

> *For whoever has will be given more, and they will have an abundance. Whoever does not have, even what they have will be taken from them.*

> Matthew 25:29

Jesus spoke about the rewards of a trustworthy servant in Luke 19:

> *He was made king, however, and returned home. Then he sent for the servants to whom he had given the money, in order to find out what they had gained with it.*

> *The first one came and said, "Sir, your mina has earned ten more."*

> *"Well done, my good servant!" his master replied. "Because you have been trustworthy in*

a very small matter, take charge of ten cities."

vs 15-17

Here a servant has been faithful with a little bit of money and as a result, he is given ten cities. I love the potential effect of that: Whoever learns to steward the jobs, finances, and abilities given to him, and diligently applies himself to learn how to generate an increase, he will be trusted to administer the fullness of the Kingdom of God in greater arenas. For some, that may include governing cities and nations because they understand that God designed jobs for them that exercise kingly thinking and teach lessons about the character of perseverance, tenacity, and being faithful. Those who do not learn these lessons of managing their "worldly wealth" and abilities are considered "not trustworthy" and more often than not, they will be stuck in the boring cycle of being preoccupied with merely trying to survive in life.

So if you have not been trustworthy in handling worldly wealth, who will trust you with true riches?

Luke 16:11

Learning to properly manage and administer what we have been allotted is not an option for those who serve the King; it is mandatory.

Kingdom Riches

Work comes to those who do their job with an abundant and prosperous kingly mindset of expansion, increase, and creative productivity, yet all the while remaining loyally conscientious. As we do, more will be added, and more, and more . . . the abundance of the King will be activated with each endeavor and its result will be multiplied again and again. Our work ignites Heaven's manifold blessing upon *all* we do.

Paul directs our sights to be set upon a vital element of our inheritance:

> *I pray that the eyes of your heart may be enlightened in order that you may know the hope to which he has called you, the riches of his glorious inheritance in his holy people.*
>
> Ephesians 1:18

The "riches of His glorious inheritance in the saints" points to all the wonderful resources God put inside each one of us: healing, encouragement, mercy, giving, prophecy, counsel, helps ministry, prayer, etc. Tapping into these riches buried within each unique person in the Body will activate the inheritance Jesus intends His church to manifest. The key to learning how to mine and disseminate these resources in a way that will produce the work of Heaven and result in true riches with an eternal reward, is found in learning how to manage and develop their full measure and potential. I believe the first step is establishing and maintaining a culture of honor within the community—a healthy environment of love, friendship, respect, and encouragement. It is the fuel of Heaven for maturity and a catalyst of creative inspiration and wisdom to fulfill the mandate upon that Body.

As you develop your own resources for the Body, increasing more and more in your gifts and abilities, you'll discover that you are no longer at the mercy of societal demands nor are you subject to or limited by the economy, your salary, your upbringing, your past, your present employment, bosses, promotions, demotions, or any such thing. Rather, you are taking your talents and skills to the next level of increased abundance because you are well established in your community and walk confidently in the empowerment of His Spirit. You know who you are, and you've begun to think, act, and manage your affairs like a king. As a result, the King of kings can entrust you with true riches and provides multiple opportunities for you to influence history in this generation.

To this end I have committed to spend my life.

QUESTIONS TO PONDER

In conclusion, consider the following questions. Ask God for creative ideas and partner with Him for wisdom and strategy.

1. What is your job (or jobs)?

_____

_____

2. Do you have a stream (or streams) of income? If so, what is it?

_____

_____

3. Could you develop more resources for income? If so, how?

_____

_____

4. What do you do to make money?

_____

_____

5. What is your line of work presently?

_____

_____

6. Looking at your job, your work, your creative skills, and other abilities and experiences, how could you develop passive income and other income? (Example: write a book, sell products online, teach a class based on your job training and/or life experiences, offer your services in the community or online, etc.)

_____

_____

7. Looking forward, do you need to be trained in the direction where you're headed? What are the first steps you can begin toward these goals?

_____

_____

_____

_____

_____

_____

ENDNOTES

[1] Wilkerson, Pastor David; Sherrill, John and Elizabeth. *The Cross and the Switchblade.* Pyramid Communications, copyright 1962.

[2] Hebrew-Chaldee Gesenius, Strong's Hebrew Lexicon, #H6033, *"anah".*

[3] See John 1:46.

[4] Strong's Greek Lexicon, #G5532, *"chreia".*

[5] See Psa 50:10.

[6] See Luke 9:58.

[7] See Matt 2:7.

[8] Strong's Greek Lexicon, #G4145, *"plousios".*

[9] See Josh 1:7.

[10] See Exod 14:15.

[11] See 2 Sam 23:8-39.

[12] Strong's Hebrew Lexicon, #H2600, *"chinnam".*

[13] Strong's Greek Lexicon, #G5532, *"chreia".*

[14] Strong's Greek Lexicon, #G4137, *"pleroo".*

ABOUT THE AUTHOR

Keith Ferrante is a prophetic voice who travels internationally speaking in churches, conferences, ministry schools, and other venues. He carries a message of freedom for the Body of Christ helping to bring revival and reformation. He is a prophetic voice who carries a breaker anointing to open up the heavens and brings timely corporate and personal prophetic words. Keith has developed many resources that offer a fresh perspective on the prophetic, supernatural Kingdom-character, and spiritual gifting. Keith is passionate to see the fullness of Heaven's atmosphere here on earth and brings people into divine reality through joyful glory encounters, impartation, and signs and wonders.

Keith is the founder and director of Emerging Prophets, a ministry that provides resources for highly gifted prophetic individuals. The ministry helps them discover whether or not they are a prophet, what kind of a prophet they are, and provides resources and lessons that help develop the much-needed character to move from the calling of prophet to the office of prophet.

Keith is also a prophetic life consultant, assisting highly motivated individuals and influencers to achieve breakthrough in their personal and spiritual life, business, and position of influence.

EMERGING PROPHET SCHOOL

If you are interested in developing your prophetic call or discovering if you are a prophet, visit our website to find out how you can sign up for a module on our online school or attend a regional Emerging Prophet school near you. If you are interested in personally being developed as an emerging prophet, we also offer coaching for developing prophets, as well as marketplace leaders. If you are interested in hosting an Emerging Prophet weekend intensive to introduce the concept of developing prophets in your area, please contact us. Also if you are interested in starting an Emerging Prophet School in your area, we would love to chat with you.

If you would like to host Keith Ferrante or one of the Emerging Prophet trainers to minister in your area, please contact us at:

www.emergingprophets.com

MORE RESOURCES FROM KEITH FERRANTE

Books
- *The Happy Prophet*
- *Embracing the Emerging Prophets*
- *There Must Be More*
- *Keys to Abundance*
- *Restoring the Father's Heart*
- *Reforming the Church From a House to a Home*
- *Emerging Prophets: Discovering Your Identity Workbook*
- *Emerging Prophets: Discovering Your Metron Workbook*
- *Emerging Prophets: Calling to Office Discovery Workbook*

Music CDs
- "Unveiled Mysteries"
- "Where You Are"
- "New Sounds"
- "Falling into You"
- "Songs From Heaven"

Available at our website:

www.emergingprophets.com

Made in the USA
San Bernardino, CA
04 March 2019